Schmuck-Kunst im Jugendstil

Art Nouveau Jewellery

Tucson 2000

Dear Lilian and Derek,

As we just witnessed the end of a century
this book may show you and inspirate us
how the symbols in jewelery are still transformed
Peacocks, owls animated nature etc is
the playground for our phantasies and dreams
as it was for the great forerunners of
this books, our grandparents in fabulous
jewelry design

Lilian Gerg

Lalique

Fouquet

Gautrait

FRITZ FALK

Gaillard

Schmuck-Kunst im Jugendstil
Art Nouveau Jewellery

Vever

Wolfers

Masriera

von Cranach

ARNOLDSCHE

Copyright © by ARNOLDSCHE und
Schmuckmuseum Pforzheim

Konzeption · Concept
Fritz Falk

Mitarbeit · Assistance
Heide Nies, Cornelie Holzach

Englische Übersetzung · English translation
Joan Clough, München

Graphische Gestaltung · Layout
Silke Nalbach, Marion Ziegler, Stuttgart

Offset-Reproduktionen · Offset-Reproductions
Konzept Satz und Repro, Stuttgart

Druck · Printing
Offizin Andersen Nexö, Leipzig

**Dieses Buch wurde gedruckt auf 100% chlorfrei gebleichtem
Papier und entspricht damit dem TCF-Standard.**

This book has been printed on paper that is 100% free of chlo-
rine bleach in conformity with TCF standards.

Die Deutsche Bibliothek – CIP-Einheitsaufnahme

Schmuck-Kunst im Jugendstil: Lalique, Fouquet, Gautrait,
Gaillard, Vever, Wolfers, Masriera, von Cranach = Art Nouveau
Jewellery / Fritz Falk. [Mitarb. Heide Nies; Cornelie Holzach.
Engl. Übers. Joan Clough]. – Stuttgart: ARNOLDSCHE, 1999

ISBN 3-925369-84-8

Made in Europe, 1999

Frontispiz · Frontispiece
Innenansicht des Ladengeschäftes von Georges Fouquet
Interior of Georges Fouquet's shop

FÜR ANNA

Bildnachweis · Photo credits:
Amsterdam, Rijksmuseum-Stichting, Seiten/pages 46, 67 · Amsterdam, B.v. Bussel, Seite/page 100 · Barcelona, M. Casanelles
i Rahola, Seiten/pages 112–121, 123–126 · Berlin, Kunstgewerbemuseum, Fotostudio Hans-Joachim Bartsch, Seiten/pages
134/135 · Brüssel, Acte-Expo a.s.b.l., Seiten/pages 101, 104–
108 · Brüssel, Éditions Racine, Paul Louis, Seite/page 98 ·
Darmstadt, Hessisches Landesmuseum, Seiten/pages 47, 56,
70/71, 74 · Hamburg, Museum für Kunst und Gewerbe, Maria
Thurn, Seite/page 88 · Karlsruhe, Badisches Landesmuseum,
Seiten/pages 55, 76/77 · Lissabon, Fundação Calouste Gulben-
kian, Reinaldo Vilgas, Seite/page 24 · London, Victoria &
Albert Museum Picture Library, Seiten/pages 26, 36, 42/43 ·
München, Bayerisches Nationalmuseum, Seiten/pages 18, 19,
27, 57, 69, 138 · München, Bruno Haberland, Seiten/pages 89,
122 · München, Hemmerle Juweliere, Seiten/pages 30/31 ·
Paris, Musée des Arts Décoratifs, Service photographique,
Seiten/pages 17, 20/21, 25, 28, 29, 41, 50, 82, 84–86, 93–95 ·
Paris, Musée du Petit Palais, Photothèque des Musées de la
Ville de Paris, Seiten/pages 37–40, 45, 48, 90/91 · Pforzheim,
Schmuckmuseum Pforzheim, Günter Meyer, Seiten/pages 16,
22, 23, 32, 44, 49, 54, 61, 66, 72, 78 unten, 83, 87, 96, 102,
131, 132 · Pforzheim, Günter Meyer, Seiten/pages 130, 133,
136, 137 · Schwäbisch Gmünd, Museum Schwäbisch Gmünd,
Seite/page 60 · Stuttgart, Württembergisches Landesmuseum,
Seiten/pages 58/59, 92 · Wien, MAK – Österreichisches Mu-
seum für angewandte Kunst, Seiten/pages 68, 73, 75, 78 oben

Reproduktionen · Reproductions:
Els Masriera, Barcelona 1996, Seiten/pages 12, 110, 111 · Les
Fouquet, Paris 1983, Seiten/pages 2, 35 · Loïe Fuller, München
1995, Seiten/pages 7, 9 · Paris – Belle Epoque, Essen 1994,
Seite/page 11 · Pariser Schmuck, München 1989, Seite/page 34
· Philippe und Marcel Wolfers, Zürich 1983, Seite/page 98 ·
Philippe & Marcel Wolfers, o.O. 1992, Seite/page 99 · The
Jewels of Lalique, Paris 1998, Seiten/pages 14, 15 · Zierkämme
und ornamentaler Haarschmuck aus Japan, Pforzheim 1978,
Seiten/pages 64, 65

Inhaltsverzeichnis · Contents

Einführung

Fritz Falk

Nur wenige Jahre blühte – in Frankreich als Art Nouveau, in Deutschland als Jugendstil bezeichnet – eine Bewegung in Kunst, Kunsthandwerk und Architektur, die mit der Pariser Weltausstellung 1900 ihren Höhepunkt erreichte. Im Gegensatz zum Historismus, der während der zweiten Hälfte des 19. Jahrhunderts Stil- und Ornamentformen längst vergangener Epochen neu belebt hatte, fand die »neue Kunst« ihre Vorbilder in der Natur: Der Mensch, das Tier und die Pflanze dienten in ornamentaler Verwandlung als die Motive, die – oft symbolistisch befrachtet – Voraussetzungen boten für eine die Belle Epoque und das Fin de Siècle bestimmende Kunst.

Neben der Bildhauerei, der Malerei und den grafischen Künsten war es vor allem das Kunsthandwerk, in dem sich die neuen Ideen manifestierten: Möbel, Glaskunst, Keramik und Porzellan, Kleinplastik, Silberschmiedekunst und der Schmuck wurden ausdrucksvolle Träger des neuen Stiles, dessen Wurzeln bei den präraffaelitischen Künstlern der Mitte des 19. Jahrhunderts und bei dem in den 70er Jahren einsetzenden Japonismus, der Auseinandersetzung Europas mit der Kunst des alten Japan, zu finden sind.

Als überragende Persönlichkeit mit geradezu unerschöpflicher Kreativität und einzigartigem handwerklichem Können gehört der Goldschmied René Lalique noch heute zu den herausragenden Künstlern des französischen Jugendstils. Er gilt zurecht als der Erneuerer der Schmuckkunst, der mit seinen phantasievollen Kreationen auf der *Exposition Universelle* 1900 wahre Triumphe feierte. In seinem Œuvre gipfelte die neue Schmuckkunst der Belle Epoque.

Neben Lalique erwuchs aus der Tradition der berühmten Pariser Juweliere der Schmuckkünstler Georges Fouquet, dem Lucien Gaillard mit seinen filigranen Haarsteckern und Zierkämmen nicht nachsteht. Léopold Gautrait setzte das Tier, mit Vorliebe den Vogel, als zentrales Motiv für seine Schmuckstücke ein. In der Maison Vever kamen neben Paul und Henri Vever auch andere Entwerfer zum Zuge, die gemeinsam den Stil dieses renommierten Hauses · prägten. Paris und Nancy waren die Zentren des Art Nouveau in Frankreich. Barcelona kennt als

Blick auf das Weltausstellungsgelände Paris 1900

View of the 1900 Paris Exhibition

katalanische Variante den Modernismo, der mit Lluis Masriera einen außergewöhnlichen Schmuckkünstler hervorbrachte. In Brüssel fand der belgische Jugendstilschmuck seinen Protagonisten in Philippe Wolfers, während in Berlin mit Wilhelm Lucas von Cranach ein Künstler tätig war, der in seinen Schmuckentwürfen frei mit den Art Nouveau-Einflüssen aus Paris spielte.

Nahezu alles, was Kunst und Kunsthandwerk des Art Nouveau anbieten, kann unter den Begriff des *Symbolismus* gestellt werden. Es ist nicht nur die äußere Form, die ein Produkt prägt: Vielfach sind es die Inhalte, die einen Gegenstand kunsthandwerklichen Schaffens in eine die Form überhöhende Dimension heben.

Die offensichtliche Gestalt der Dinge verschafft dem Betrachter ein ästhetisches Vergnügen; eine andere den Gläsern, den Vasen, den Möbeln und den Schmuckstücken innewohnende Kraft erschließt sich dem Kenner durch Wissen, das viele Aspekte umfaßt: alte und zeitgenössische Dichtkunst und Literatur, antike und moderne Mythologien, Märchen und Sagen, neueste Erfahrungen philosophischen Denkens und vieles mehr. Die Bedürfnisse sind verschieden. Dem einen genügt die reine Freude, die er empfindet, wenn er das Werk betrachtet und aus der Form, den Farben, auch aus der handwerklichen Perfektion seinen Genuß zieht. Für den anderen ist es unabdingbar, alle Hintergründe zu kennen. Nur dann erschließt sich für ihn eine *Ganzheit*.

Kaum ein Motiv, mit dem sich die Künstler des Art Nouveau befaßten, steht nur als Form alleine. Häufig – nicht ausschließlich –

stößt man bei der Betrachtung der Werke gerade der französischen Schmuckkünstler dann, wenn es sich um die figural-ornamentale Richtung des Jugendstils handelt, auf Vorbilder, die in ihrer Verwandlung zum Schmuckstück bei höchster ästhetischer Qualität symbolische Inhalte in sich tragen oder literarische Aussagen machen.

Die äußere Form fast aller Goldschmiedearbeiten des Art Nouveau ist abgeleitet von der Natur in ihren vielfältigen Erscheinungsweisen: Tiere, Pflanzen, Menschen, Landschaft, Wasser. Es ist jedoch keine sklavische Abhängigkeit der Kunstform vom natürlichen Vorbild. Für kurze Zeit stand ein metamorphosisches Prinzip im Vordergrund. Das natürliche Vorbild erfuhr wie nie zuvor eine fließend-ornamentale Verwandlung: spannungsvolles Ausschwingen und Zurückgleiten von anschwellenden und ausklingenden Linien, am natürlichen Vorbild sich orientierend und doch frei damit spielend.

Es gibt Formen in der Natur, die sich im Sinne des Art Nouveau geradezu anbieten zur Umwandlung ins Ornament. Blüten und Blätter mancher Blumen gehören ebenso dazu wie Vögel und Insekten, deren wirkliche und allegorische Leichtigkeit sie zu Prototypen des Jugendstils werden lassen. Gestalt und Antlitz des Menschen, fast ausschließlich der Frau, bieten in Zartheit und Eleganz ästhetische Voraussetzungen, die die Künstler in tanzgleichem Fluß der Linien nutzten. Die Landschaft, Seen und Berge erfahren ihre Umsetzung nicht zuletzt durch die Raffinesse der hierfür eingesetzten Werkstoffe – die Metalle, das Email,

Félix Vallotton, Plakat für
L'Art Nouveau, 1895
Museum für Kunst und Gewerbe,
Hamburg

Félix Vallotton, poster for
L'Art Nouveau, 1895

die Edelsteine, die Perlen, auch die im Jugendstilschmuck neuartigen Materialien wie Elfenbein, Schildpatt, Horn und Glas.

Die Gründerjahre, die politisch und ökonomisch die zweite Hälfte des 19. Jahrhunderts prägten, hatten die Welt verändert. Kunst und Kultur blickten historisierend zurück und zugleich bahnbrechend in die Zukunft. Europa hatte sich machtbesessen »die Erde untertan« gemacht: in Afrika und Asien waren Kolonien eingerichtet worden. Japan öffnete sich nach jahrhundertelanger Isolation und überraschte die westliche Welt mit seiner Geschichte und Kunst.

Diese erste Internationalisierung der Welt mit ihren Einflüssen aus bisher weitgehend unbekannten Kulturen war faszinierend für eine Elite von Dichtern und Philosophen, für bildende Künstler und Musiker, für Wissenschaftler und auch für die Vertreter der angewandten Künste, die sich den neuen Anregungen öffneten und neue Erkenntnisse in neuartigen Zusammenhängen suchten.

Charles Baudelaires *Blumen des Bösen* waren zwar schon 1857 erschienen, hatten ihre Wirkung zu Ende des Jahrhunderts jedoch noch keineswegs eingebüßt. Paul Verlaine veröffentlichte seine *Confession* 1895; er gilt als der herausragende Repräsentant des literarischen Symbolismus. Oscar Wilde brachte 1893 seine *Salomé* auf die Bühne, Sarah Bernhardt triumphierte im Pariser Theater und die amerikanische Tänzerin Loïe Fuller faszinierte mit ihren symbolträchtigen Schleiertänzen ihr Publikum. In Wien machte Sigmund Freud mit seinen tiefenpsychologischen Studien auf sich aufmerksam, und Wilhelm Röntgen ermöglichte 1895 mit den nach ihm benannten Strahlen einen ganz anderen Blick in das Innere des Menschen.

Die Malerei befreite sich aus vielerlei Zwängen: Claude Monet malte die Blumen in Gärten und Teichen, Paul Gauguin fand seine künstlerische Reife in exotischen Welten voll symbolischer Anspielungen, Odilon Redon verflocht sich und seine Kunst in einem phantastischen Symbolismus.

Die angewandte Kunst hat ihre eigenen Gesetze. Sie ist konkret auf den Menschen gerichtet, sie dient ihm durch ihre Funktion. Der Schmuck findet seine Aufgabe in der Selbstdarstellung des Individuums, er ist ein Zeichen, durch das sich Trägerin und Träger in ihren Persönlichkeiten verwirklichen können. Auch der Schmuckgestalter stellt sich dar in seiner künstlerischen Individualität, als Repräsentant seiner Zeit, der eingebunden ist in den »Zeitgeist«, der ihn beeinflußt und den er mitgestaltet.

Die Tiere, die Pflanzen, der Mensch werden nicht abgebildet, sondern transformiert und mit Symbolwerten belegt. Sie können Zartheit und Brutalität versinnbildlichen. Blumen wie Orchidee, Lotos, Lilie, Iris und Mohn erscheinen als Symbole und Attribute der Frau, Pfauen und Schwäne charakterisieren Mut, Würde, Eitelkeit, Reinheit und Grazie. Leicht erkennbar oder verborgen sind die Symbole, aussagekräftig im Zusammenspiel mit dem Sinngehalt der Edelsteine und Perlen, der Farben und Transparenz des Emails.

Zu entdecken und verstehen gibt es vieles im Schmuck von Jugendstil und Art Nouveau.

Jules Cheret, Folies-Bergère. Loïe Fuller, 1897

Introduction

Fritz Falk

The movement known in France as Art Nouveau and in Germany as Jugendstil flowered in the brief space of ten years, culminating in the 1900 Paris Exhibition. In the later half of the 19th century, Historicism represented a revival of period styles and decorative forms from epochs long past. By contrast, Art Nouveau, 'New Art', was modelled on nature. The human form, flora and fauna were changed into decorative shapes and translated into motifs which were often loaded with symbolic connotations reflecting the Fin de Siècle spirit of the times.

New ideas created an environment in which the applied and decorative arts as well as the fine arts flourished. Furniture, glass, china and porcelain, small-scale sculpture, silver objets de vertu and, most importantly, jewellery, expressed the new style. Its roots went back to the mid-19th century Pre-Raphaelite movement in England and the Japonisme which set in during the 1870s, when Europe became enamoured of Japanese art.

The French goldsmith René Lalique is still regarded as the leading exponent of Art Nouveau. Boundlessly creative and blessed with a teeming imagination, he was both designer and craftsman. His innovative jewellery design was the hit of the Paris *Exposition Universelle,* catapulting him to instant and lasting fame. His oeuvre represents the best in Belle Époque jewellery.

Lalique was surrounded by brilliant contemporaries. Georges Fouquet was the son of a highly successful Paris goldsmith and jeweller. Lucien Gaillard was celebrated for exquisitely delicate hair ornaments and combs and Léopold Gautrait designed jewellery around animal motifs, particularly birds. Both Fouquet and Maison Vever, headed by Paul and Henri Vever, launched jewellery designers who collaborated with the firms to become famous under their own names. Paris and Nancy were the centres of Art Nouveau jewellery making in France. Barcelona produced a Catalan variant in Modernismo. Its leading exponent was Lluis Masriera, a superb craftsman and jewellery designer. Belgian Art Nouveau was represented by Philippe Wolfers in Brussels. In Wilhelm Lucas von Cranach Berlin possessed a distinctively macabre designer who went well beyond the aesthetic currents prevailing in Paris.

Art Nouveau art and art objects lend themselves to broader classification under the heading of *Symbolism.* Both content and external form denote the product, be it made of glass, china, metal, wood or fabric. The cryptic meaning, symbolically expressed, is what elevates an object made by an Art Nouveau artisan to a plane transcending form.

The shape of things is what attracts attention. Connoisseurs, of course, know what is aesthetically satisfying about a glass, a vase, a piece of furniture or jewellery. To understand why something is aesthetically satisfying one must command broad-ranging knowledge encompassing both subject matter and overarching thematic content. Connoisseurs ideally draw on ancient and modern poetry and letters, ancient and modern mythologies, fairy tales and legends, philosophy ancient and contemporary, in short on cultural material from all corners of the earth.

Our aesthetic needs differ. Some people are content with merely enjoying what they feel when looking at an art object. This approach is based on pleasure in shapes, forms and colours or simply on appreciation of superb craftsmanship. Other people, and there is no getting round this, simply must know everything there is to know about the background of the object they are interested in. Then, and only then, can art lovers belonging to this group feel that they are grasping an object as an *aesthetic entity.*

Art Nouveau motifs rarely stand alone on their own merits as pure form. Sometimes, and this is particularly true of French Art Nouveau jewellery design of the figurative-ornamental School, one immediately realizes that the transformation of natural forms into jewellery of the highest aesthetic standard has endowed them with symbolic content and even the power of making a literary statement.

Nearly all shapes typical of Art Nouveau gold jewellery derive from natural phenomena: animals, plants, people, landscape, water. The new forms thus derived are not slavish copies of nature. They have undergone a complete metamorphosis into ornamental fluidity of line, in shapes both vegetal and free-form. Stringent elegance is combined with sinuous curvilinear opulence. Thus evoked, nature is still eloquent in transformation.

Some natural shapes seem to have been ideally suited to transformation into Art Nouveau ornament. Flowering plants, blossoms, buds and flower petals. The lightness of being inherent in birds and insects, flying and flight

as such, have made them the archetypes of Jugendstil and Art Nouveau on both the real and the allegorical plane. The delicacy and elegance of an idealized female face and figure lent themselves superbly to the dancing fluidity of line with which Art Nouveau artists configured spirit in free fall. Art Nouveau designers transmuted landscapes, lakes and mountains into new forms via the sophisticated redeployment of metals, both rare and base, some of them new to the art of jewellery design in the West like ivory, tortoiseshell, horn and glass.

The heady years of rapid industrial expansion in Europe and especially Germany after 1871 represented an era that changed the world politically, economically and aesthetically. Art and culture in the broader sense of the term were retro, looking back to sum up the past. However, they also looked forward. Obsessed with global domination, Europe established colonies throughout Africa and Asia. Japan, on the other hand, opened its doors to the West after centuries of voluntary isolation, dazzling Europe with its art.

This first period of globalisation, drawing as it did on cultures which had been previously unknown, fascinated a European élite of poets, philosophers, artists, musicians, scientists and scholars, not least among them the leading protagonists of the decorative and applied arts. Everyone was open to new sources of inspiration and eager to broaden their horizons.

Charles Baudelaire's *Les Fleurs du Mal* was published in 1857 but had lost nothing of its initial impact by the end of the 19th century. Paul Verlaine's *Confession* appeared in print in 1895. Today he is regarded as the leading exponent of literary Symbolism. Oscar Wilde's *Salome* was staged in a lavish production. Sarah Bernhardt triumphed in Paris theatre and the American dancer Loïe Fuller enchanted Paris audiences with performances literally veiled in Symbolism. In Vienna Sigmund Freud was becoming famous for his studies of the workings of the unconscious. In 1895 Wilhelm Röntgen discovered the rays named in German after him (X-rays). Between them they made the inner being transparent.

Painting liberated itself from constraints which had shackled it in the past. Claude Monet painted flowers in gardens and on ponds. Paul Gauguin became a mature artist in real and symbolic realms. Odilon Redon wove himself and his art into a fantastic fabric of Symbolism.

The applied and decorative arts are a law unto themselves. First, they are aimed at us and their function is to serve us. The function of jewellery is to allow people wearing it to express their personalities. Wearing jewellery is a sign that one is becoming self-actualized. In designing and making jewellery, goldsmiths also reveal their distinctive personalities both as artists and as representatives of their times. The 'Zeitgeist' exerts a formative influence on them and they in turn shape it in their work.

Animal, plant and human motifs in Art Nouveau jewellery are not representational. They represent transformation of form through the addition of symbolic content. Thus transmuted, they symbolize or personify delicacy or brutality. Flowers like the orchid, lotus, lily, iris and poppy appeared in Art Nouveau jewellery as symbols and as attributes of idealized woman. Peacocks and swans represented positive traits like courage and dignity, purity and grace as well as negative ones like vanity. These symbolic connotations represent forceful aesthetic statements when combined with the historical meanings associated with the properties of precious stones, pearls and enamel, their colours and translucency.

There is so much to discover and understand in Jugendstil and Art Nouveau jewellery.

**Lluis Masriera, Anhänger »Nymphe«,
Barcelona 1908**

Lluis Masriera, "Nymph" pendant,
Barcelona 1908

René Lalique

René Lalique

René Lalique (1860–1945)

Als Goldschmied im traditionellen Sinne wurde er ausgebildet, zu einer Zeit, als Realismus, Naturalismus und Historismus die Kunst und das Kunsthandwerk prägten. Als Erneuerer, der die alte Handwerkskunst des Goldschmiedens perfekt beherrschte, der neue Techniken erfand und weiterentwickelte, der für die Herstellung von Schmuckstücken bisher eher ungewöhnliche Werkstoffe in seine Kreationen einbezog, der die symbolistisch-literarischen, die künstlerischen und wohl auch die musikalischen Strömungen seiner Zeit kannte und diese wie kein anderer zuvor für seinen Schmuck als Quellen der Inspiration zu nutzen verstand, ging René Lalique in die Geschichte der Schmuckkunst ein.

Ausgestattet mit höchster Empfindsamkeit schuf Lalique, der schon als Kind der Natur eng verbunden war, eine Schmuckkunst, die in der ornamentalen Verwandlung natürlicher Vorbilder ebenso wie in der Umsetzung symbolistischer und literarischer Vorlagen ihre Vollendung fand: In der Gestalt und im Antlitz des Menschen und in den vielfältigen Erscheinungsweisen der Tiere und Pflanzen, vornehmlich der Vögel und Insekten sowie unterschiedlichster Blumen und Blüten.

Viele der von Lalique geschaffenen Kleinodien, oft und gerade in der Kombination unterschiedlicher Motive – Frau und Insekt zum Beispiel bei der einzigartigen *Libellenfrau* im Calouste Gulbenkian Museum in Lissabon – spiegeln gesellschaftliche, kulturelle und auch politische Situationen der Jahrhundertwende wider, die in Dichtung und Musik, in Kunst und Wissenschaft nach-

haltig von Extremen und Widersprüchen geprägt waren: von Lebenslust und Ekel, von Zuversicht in ein neues Jahrhundert und von Ängsten davor, von Ernsthaftigkeit und Zynismus, Spott und Ironie.

Laliques Kreativität, die die natürlichen Vorbilder in ornamentale Schwingungen umzusetzen verstand, ohne dabei die charakteristischen Werte aufzugeben, war die Voraussetzung für den triumphalen Erfolg, der seinen Höhepunkt 1900 auf der *Exposition Universelle* hatte. Nicht minder hoch anzusetzen ist Laliques Verständnis für die Eigenfarbigkeit seiner Motive und sein Vermögen, die natürlichen Farben umzusetzen und in seinem Werk wirkungsvoll zu kombinieren: bläulich-schimmernde Mondsteine und mattweißes Glas zur Wiedergabe von Weidenknospen und Zweigen, symbolträchtiges kraftvolles Blau, um geradezu tiefgründig erotische Symbolkraft in Email auszudrücken.

Ein weiteres kam hinzu: Lalique hatte in dem kunstverständigen Erdölmagnaten Calouste Sarkis Gulbenkian einen leidenschaftlichen Verehrer und potenten Mäzen gefunden. Dieser ermöglichte es Lalique, völlig unabhängig die phantastischen Kreationen zu schaffen, die seine Genialität erst voll zur Geltung brachten.

Mit seinen Mitteln und auf seine Weise war René Lalique Beobachter und Mitgestalter der Belle Époque, auch des Aufbruchs in das 20. Jahrhundert. Zweifellos war er, der große Anreger, der hochgepriesene Goldschmied, eine der herausragenden Künstlerpersönlichkeiten seiner Zeit.

René Lalique

René Lalique trained as a goldsmith under Louis Aucoc when the fine and applied arts were under the sway of Naturalism and Historicism. A versatile innovator, he was the supreme master of his craft. Inventing new techniques and continuing to develop them, Lalique introduced materials which had never before been used in Western jewellery. Moreover, Lalique was the first jewellery designer to draw on *Symbolism* in literature, the fine and applied arts and even music for his inspired creations. In all senses of the word, he wrote history in Art Nouveau jewellery design.

Lalique was an extremely sensitive person. One cannot imagine him as anything else when one looks at his exquisite brooches, pendants, necklaces, rings and tiaras. A lifelong love of nature inspired Lalique to the innovative translation of natural motifs into matchless ornamental form. The female figure and face, flora – flowers, buds and plants – and fauna, especially birds and insects, were suffused in his hands with symbolic symbolism.

Many of the jewels created by Lalique represent distinctive combinations of motifs like the unique *Dragonfly Lady,* who is both woman and insect, in the Calouste Gulbenkian Museum in Lisbon. These creations are not merely art for art's sake. On the contrary, they are conscious reflections of the social, cultural and political context of late 19th and early 20th-century Europe. The Fin de Siècle was a time fraught with extreme tensions: joie de vivre and disgust, confidence in what the new century would bring and fear of what might come. Intellectual posturing and expressed emotions fluctuated between seriousness and cynicism, mockery and irony.

Lalique's brilliance and his vivid imagination enabled him to turn natural shapes into decoratively sinuous motifs which, in being translated into jewellery design, lost none of their inherent aesthetic qualities. Beginning with his triumph at the 1900 Paris *Exposition Universelle,* Lalique knew how to capitalize on his success and remained triumphantly ahead of his contemporaries in all materials and media he subsequently dealt with. He knew how to use the colour values of his natural models, translating them into stunning new combinations. Shimmering moonstones were worked with matte white glass to represent willow buds and twigs. Bright blue enamel became a colour loaded with historic symbolism evocative of profound eroticism.

Lalique was truly fortunate in finding a committed admirer and powerful patron in Calouste Sarkis Gulbenkian, the fabled oil tycoon and connoisseur of the arts. Sarah Bernhardt loved Lalique's jewellery and she presumably introduced the artist to the collector. Gulbenkian assured Lalique the financial independence that allowed him to produce his fabulous jewellery.

René Lalique was both observer and prime mover and shaker of Belle Époque design. Consequently, it can be said of him that he was instrumental in ushering in 20th-century art. A brilliant goldsmith and designer, he inspired craftsmen and subsequent movements for the rest of the 20th century.

**Sarah Bernhardt
mit Schmuck von René Lalique**

Sarah Bernhardt
wearing jewellery by René Lalique

René Lalique

Anhänger und Kette »Frauenkopf
und Kornblumen«
Gold, weißer Chalzedon, Email,
Perlen
um 1898/99
Länge des Anhängers 10,2 cm
Länge der Kette 71,6 cm
Musée des Arts Décoratifs, Paris

Pendant and chain "Lady's head and
cornflowers"
Gold, white chalcedony, enamel,
pearls
ca 1898/99
Length of pendant 10.2 cm
Length of chain 71.6 cm
Musée des Arts Décoratifs, Paris

René Lalique

Brosche »Chrysanthemen«
Gold, Diamanten, Aquamarine,
Glas, Email
vor 1903
Länge 9 cm
Schmuckmuseum Pforzheim

Brooch "Chrysanthemums"
Gold, diamonds, aquamarines,
glass, enamel
before 1903
Length 9 cm
Schmuckmuseum Pforzheim

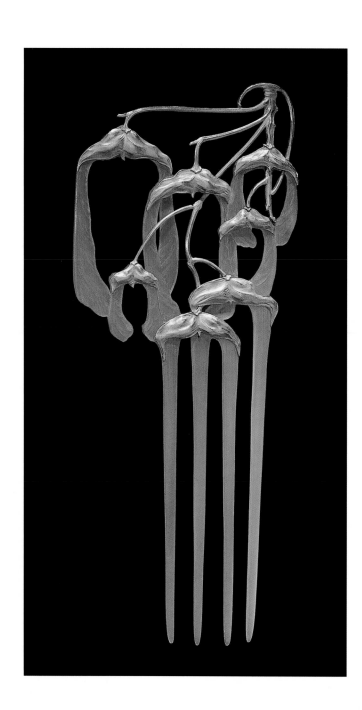

René Lalique

Schmuckkamm »Ahornfrüchte«
Horn, Gold
um 1902/03
Höhe 15,9 cm
Bayerisches Nationalmuseum,
München

Ornamental comb "Maple seeds"
Horn, gold
ca 1902/03
Height 15.9 cm
Bayerisches Nationalmuseum,
Munich

René Lalique

Haarstecker »Hortensie und Biene«
Horn, Gold, Glas, Opal, Email
um 1902
Höhe 16,3 cm
Bayerisches Nationalmuseum,
München

Hairpin "Hydrangea and bee"
Horn, gold, glass, opal, enamel
ca 1902
Height 16.3 cm
Bayerisches Nationalmuseum,
Munich

René Lalique

Brosche/Anhänger
»Zwei Schwalben«
Gold, Diamanten, Email
um 1906/08
Breite 10,8 cm
Musée des Arts Décoratifs, Paris
Abb. S. 20/21

Brooch/pendant "Two swallows"
Gold, diamonds, enamel
ca 1906/1908
Width 10.8 cm
Musée des Arts Décoratifs, Paris
ill. p. 20/21

**Brosche/Anhänger »Mädchenköpfe
mit Schwalben«
Gold, Email, Perle
um 1898/1900
Breite 7 cm
Schmuckmuseum Pforzheim**

Brooch/pendant "Girls' heads with
swallows"
Gold, enamel, pearl
ca 1898/1900
Width 7 cm
Schmuckmuseum Pforzheim

René Lalique

**Anhänger »Zwei Pfauen«
Gold, Opal, Email, Perlen
um 1897/98
Breite 3,9 cm
Schmuckmuseum Pforzheim**

Pendant "Two peacocks"
Gold, opal, enamel, pearls
ca 1897/98
Width 3.9 cm
Schmuckmuseum Pforzheim

Diadem »Hahnenkopf«
Gold, Amethyst, Email, Horn
um 1897/98
Breite 15,5 cm
Calouste Gulbenkian Museum,
Lissabon

Tiara "Cock's head"
Gold, amethyst, enamel, horn
ca 1897/98
Width 15.5 cm
Calouste Gulbenkian Museum,
Lisbon

René Lalique

Anhänger/Brosche »Pfau«
Gold, Opale, Email
um 1897/98
Breite 5,6 cm
Musée des Arts Décoratifs, Paris

Pendant/brooch "Peacock"
Gold, opals, enamel
ca 1897/98
Width 5.6 cm
Musée des Arts Décoratifs, Paris

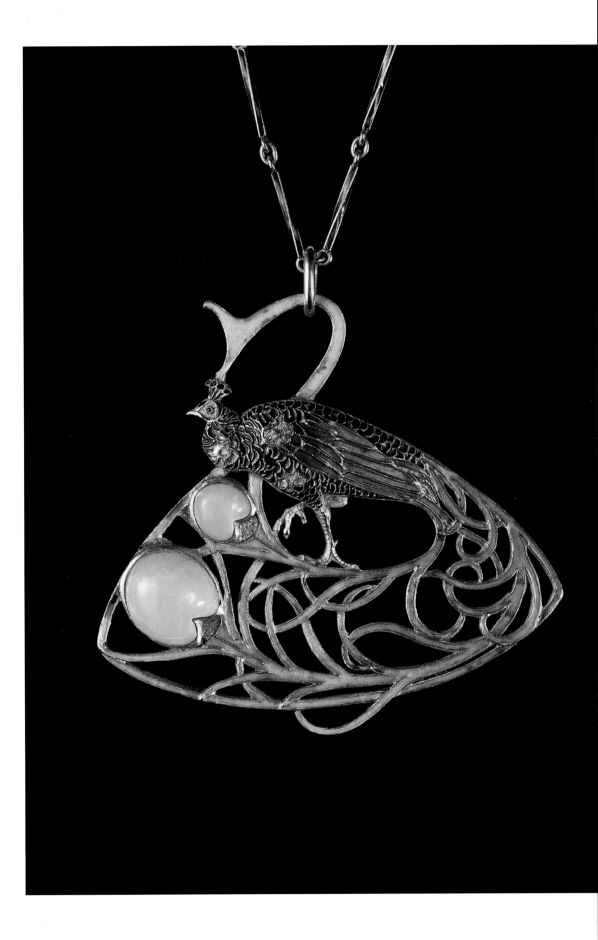

René Lalique

**Diadem und Brustschmuck
»Wickenblüten«
Gold, Glas, Topase, Email, Horn,
Schildpatt
um 1902/04
Breite des Diadems 16,4 cm
Breite des Brustschmucks 13,1 cm
The Trustees of the Victoria and
Albert Museum, London**

Tiara and bodice "Sweet peas"
Gold, glass, topazes, enamel, horn,
tortoiseshell
ca 1902/04
Width of tiara 16.4 cm
Width of bodice 13.1 cm
The Trustees of the Victoria and
Albert Museum, London

René Lalique

Anhänger »Stiefmütterchen«
Gold, Diamanten, Perle, Email
um 1900
Länge 9 cm
Bayerisches Nationalmuseum,
München

Pendant "Pansy"
Gold, diamonds, pearl, enamel
ca 1900
Length 9 cm
Bayerisches Nationalmuseum,
Munich

René Lalique

Schmuckkamm »Zwei Pfauen«
Horn patiniert, Gold, Opalscheiben
um 1897/98
Höhe 18,4 cm
Musée des Arts Décoratifs, Paris

Ornamental comb "Two peacocks"
Horn, patinated, gold, flat-cut opals
ca 1897/98
Height 18.4 cm
Musée des Arts Décoratifs, Paris

René Lalique

Brosche »Pfau«
Gold, Mondsteine, Email
um 1898/99
Breite 6 cm
Musée des Arts Décoratifs, Paris

Brooch "Peacock"
Gold, moonstones, enamel
ca 1898/99
Width 6 cm
Musée des Arts Décoratifs, Paris

René Lalique

Halsschmuck (Collier-de-chien)
»Kornblumen«
Gold, Diamanten, Email, Perlen
um 1902/03
Breite der Platte 8,2 cm
Hemmerle Juweliere, München
Abb. S. 30/31

Necklace (Collier-de-chien)
"Cornflowers"
Gold, diamonds, enamel, pearls
ca 1902/03
Width of clasp 8.2 cm
Hemmerle Juweliere, Munich
ill. p. 30/31

René Lalique

Ring »Nymphe«
Gold, Email
um 1900
Durchmesser 3,1 cm
Schmuckmuseum Pforzheim

Ring "Nymph"
Gold, enamel
ca 1900
Diameter 3.1 cm
Schmuckmuseum Pforzheim

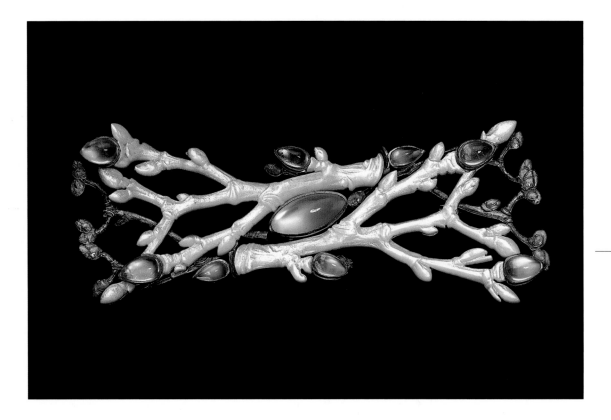

René Lalique

Brosche »Weidenzweige«
Gold, Glas, Mondsteine, Email
um 1902/04
Breite 10,1 cm
Schmuckmuseum Pforzheim

Brooch "Willow twigs"
Gold, glass, moonstones, enamel
ca 1902/04
Width 10.1 cm
Schmuckmuseum Pforzheim

Georges Fouquet

Georges Fouquet

Georges Fouquet (1862–1957)

Georges Fouquet war der Sohn des in der zweiten Hälfte des 19. Jahrhunderts erfolgreichen Pariser Juweliers und Goldschmieds Alphonse Fouquet. Damit war er entsprechend ausgebildet und stand anfänglich in der Tradition des in den väterlichen Werkstätten gepflegten historisierenden Stils der Neo-Renaissance. Als er im Jahre 1895 die Firma des Vaters übernahm, bahnte sich der Wandel im Hause Fouquet an: 1898 stellte Georges Fouquet erstmals Schmuckstücke im Stil des Art Nouveau aus, allerdings noch ohne durchschlagenden Erfolg. Die Exponate seien zu schwerfällig, meinte der Kollege und Kritiker Henri Vever.

Anläßlich der *Exposition Universelle* von 1900 änderte sich dies jedoch grundlegend. Neben Lalique war Fouquet der am meisten beachtete Aussteller von künstlerisch hochwertigem Schmuck. Die Gründe hierfür lagen einerseits in der kurz zuvor begonnenen Zusammenarbeit mit dem freiberuflich für Fouquet tätigen Entwerfer Charles Desrosiers, vorrangig aber in der Tatsache, daß es Fouquet gelungen war, den 1860 in Mähren geborenen Maler und Grafiker Alphonse Mucha für sich zu gewinnen. Mucha war in erster Linie wegen seiner Plakate berühmt geworden, hatte sich aber auch als Entwerfer für Möbel, Teppiche, Glasfenster und Theaterdekorationen hervorgetan. Seine im Hause Fouquet ausgeführten spektakulären Schmuckobjekte – eher Ausstellungsstücke als wirklich tragbare Schmuckstücke – bewirkten das enorme Aufsehen, das Fouquet auf der Weltausstellung von 1900 für sein Haus verbuchen konnte. Daß die gefeierte und skandalum-

witterte Schauspielerin Sarah Bernhardt, für die Fouquet den berühmten von Mucha entworfenen Schlangenarmreif geschaffen hatte, zu den bevorzugten Kundinnen des Hauses gehörte, trug zum hohen Ansehen Fouquets zweifellos bei.

Der Schmuck aus den Werkstätten Fouquets stammte zum einen von Georges Fouquet selbst, zum andern von Desrosiers. Dieser war Schüler von Eugène Grasset, der seinerseits für die Maison Vever tätig war. Für Fouquet arbeitete er seit Mitte der 90er Jahre. Die Kooperation dauerte zumindest bis 1903, als im Salon der Société des Artistes Français noch Schmuckstücke ausgestellt wurden, die aus der Zusammenarbeit Fouquet-Desrosiers resultierten. Weitgehend zart und subtil sind diese im Aufbau, vielgestaltig in der Verwendung pflanzlicher Vorbilder, gelegentlich auch kraftvoll und ideenreich in der Umsetzung landschaftlicher Motive wie Seen, Wasserfälle und Berge, die einen intensiven Glanz in sich tragen, wirkungsvoll unterstützt von Perlen und edlen Steinen, den oft in schmalen Stegen gefaßten kleinen Diamanten und den flachen Opalen, die so charakteristisch sind für den in Fouquets Werkstätten entstandenen Schmuck.

Die menschliche Figur und die Tiergestalt – sieht man von den theatralischen Schöpfungen, die weitgehend von Alphonse Mucha stammen, ab – haben bei Fouquet und Desrosiers eine weniger wichtige Rolle gespielt.

Georges Fouquet

Georges Fouquet was the son of the successful Paris goldsmith and jeweller Alphonse Fouquet. With such a background, Georges Fouquet was predestined to receive excellent training in his craft. He initially worked within the historicizing Neo-Renaissance style which had made his father's reputation in the latter half of the 19th century. When Georges Fouquet took over his father's business in 1895 and registered his own stamp, the House of Fouquet took a giant leap forward. Georges Fouquet first exhibited jewellery of his own design in 1898. Although it was in the early Art Nouveau style, it did not catch on. Henri Vever, a colleague and writer on the arts found Fouquet's early work singularly heavy.

The 1900 Paris Exhibition marked a sea change in Fouquet's standing as a designer and jeweller. Public and critics alike admired him for his superbly designed and crafted jewellery. Fouquet's collaboration with the freelance designer Charles Desrosiers was another reason for the upturn his firm experienced. Desrosiers continued to work for him until about 1910. He also persuaded the painter and graphic artist Alphonse Mucha to work with him, another great boost for the firm's reputation. Born in Moravia in 1860, Mucha became famous for poster designs. He also made a name for himself in designing furniture, carpets, stained-glass windows and even stage scenery. The spectacular jewellery he designed for Fouquet created a sensation at the 1900 Paris Exhibition because these were primarily beautiful pieces to be worn and not merely admired as artefacts. A further factor contributing to Fouquet's overnight rise to celebrity was Sarah Bernhardt's patronage. Mucha designed the famous snake bangle for the *femme fatale par excellence* of the Belle Époque and she bought it from Fouquet. Sarah Bernhardt's loyalty to the firm continued to enhance its reputation.

Georges Fouquet designed some of the jewellery his firm sold but much of it was made by Desrosiers. Desrosiers trained under Eugène Grasset and Grasset worked for Maison Vever. Desrosiers designed for Fouquet from the mid-1890s until 1903. During those years the Salon of the Société des Artistes Français continued to exhibit jewellery resulting from the collaboration between Fouquet and Desrosiers. At once delicate and sophisticated in design, these pieces are notable for the use of natural shapes. Many motifs were based on plants but Desrosiers also featured motifs such as lakes, waterfalls and mountains, often enamelled by Étienne Tourette. They were set to great effect with precious stones and tiny diamonds in collet mountings as well as pearls and the flat-cut opals which were a hallmark of Fouquet's ateliers.

Apart from dramatic creations after designs by Alphonse Mucha, the human or animal figure played only a minor role in the work produced by Fouquet and Desrosiers.

Entwurf von Alphonse Mucha für den »Schlangenarmreif« für Sarah Bernhardt, 1899

Design by Alphonse Mucha for "snake bangle" for Sarah Bernhardt, 1899

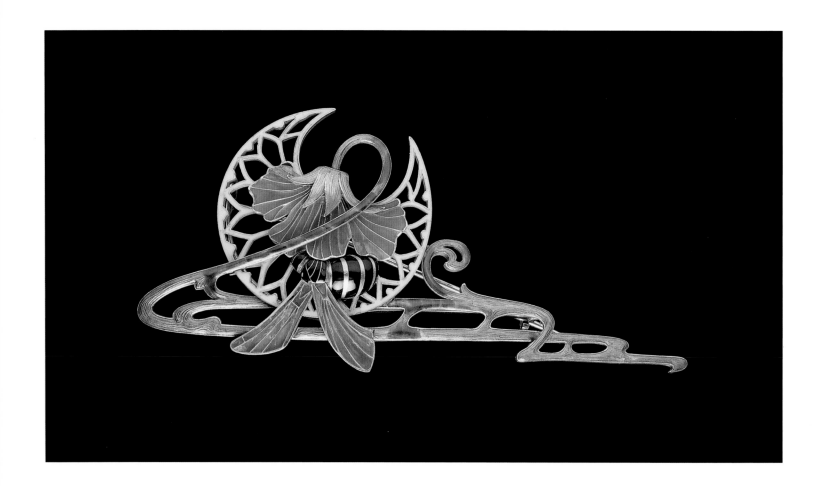

Georges Fouquet

Brosche »Hornisse«
Entwurf von Charles Desrosiers
Gold, Email
1901
Breite 13 cm
The Trustees of the Victoria and
Albert Museum, London

Brooch "Hornet"
Design Charles Desrosiers
Gold, enamel
1901
Width 13 cm
The Trustees of the Victoria and
Albert Museum, London

Georges Fouquet

Brosche »Ahornfrucht«
Gold, Diamanten, Email, Perle
zwischen 1905 und 1910
Breite 9 cm
Musée du Petit Palais, Paris

Brooch "Maple seed"
Gold, diamonds, enamel, pearl
between 1905 and 1910
Width 9 cm
Musée du Petit Palais, Paris

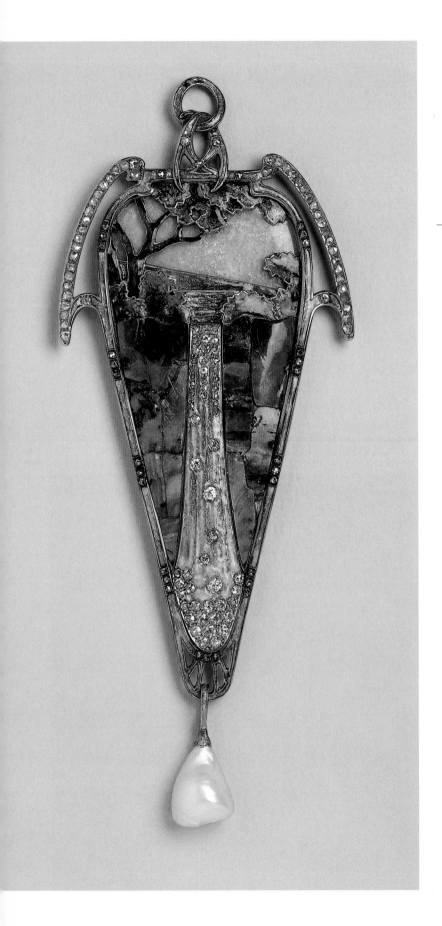

Georges Fouquet

Anhänger »Wasserfall«
Entwurf des Rahmens von
Alphonse Mucha
Entwurf des Motivs von Charles
Desrosiers
Gold, Opale, Diamanten, Email,
Perle
zwischen 1900 und 1910
Länge 12,2 cm
Musée du Petit Palais, Paris

Pendant "Cascade"
Frame design Alphonse Mucha
Motif design Charles Desrosiers
Gold, opals, diamonds, enamel,
pearl
between 1900 and 1910
Length 12.2 cm
Musée du Petit Palais, Paris

Georges Fouquet

Armreif »Distelblatt«
Entwurf von Charles Desrosiers
Gold, Opal, Email
um 1907/08
Durchmesser 6,3 cm
Musée du Petit Palais, Paris

Bracelet "Thistle leaf"
Design Charles Desrosiers
Gold, opal, enamel
ca 1907/08
Diameter 6.3 cm
Musée du Petit Palais, Paris

Georges Fouquet

Anhänger »Nelken«
Entwurf von Charles Desrosiers
Gold, Email, Diamanten, Perle
1900
Breite 5,6 cm
Musée du Petit Palais, Paris
Abb. S. 42/43

Pendant "Carnations"
Design Charles Desrosiers
Gold, enamel, diamonds, pearl
1900
Width 5.6 cm
Musée du Petit Palais, Paris
ill. p. 42/43

Georges Fouquet

Brosche »Frauenköpfe und
Mistelzweig«
Gold, Diamanten, Email, Perlen
um 1903
Breite 4,2 cm
The Trustees of the Victoria and
Albert Museum, London
Abb. S. 42/43

Brooch "Ladies' heads and mistletoe"
Gold, diamonds, enamel, pearls
ca 1903
Width 4.2 cm
The Trustees of the Victoria and
Albert Museum, London
ill. p. 42/43

Georges Fouquet

Anhänger »Kastanie«
Gold, Opale, Topase, Diamanten,
Email
1906
Breite 6 cm
Musée des Arts Décoratifs, Paris

Pendant "Chestnut"
Gold, opals, topazes, diamonds,
enamel
1906
Width 6 cm
Musée des Arts Décoratifs, Paris

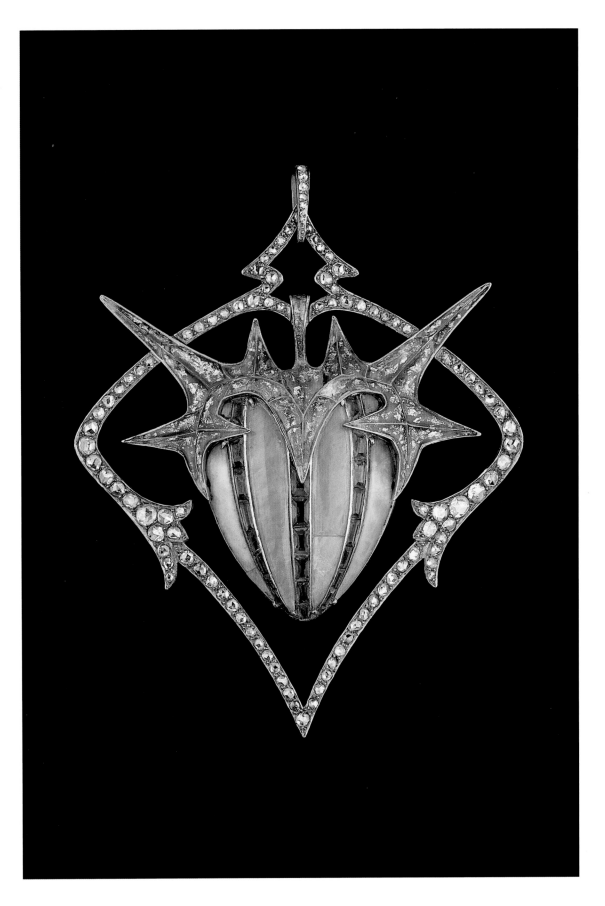

Georges Fouquet

Brosche/Anhänger »Lotos«
Gold, Diamanten, Opalmosaik,
Email, Perlen
1902
Breite 7,9 cm
Schmuckmuseum Pforzheim
(Werner Wild-Stiftung)

Brooch/pendant "Lotus"
Gold, diamonds, opal mosaic,
enamel, pearls
1902
Width 7,9 cm
Schmuckmuseum Pforzheim
(Werner Wild-Stiftung)

Diese Karte habe ich dem Buch entnommen:
In which book did you find this card?

:...

Keine Bestellung!
Schicken Sie mir bitte – unverbindlich – Informationen über
Ihr Verlagsprogramm.

This is not a purchase order!
Please send me – with no obligation – further information
on your publishing program.

Mein/e Interessengebiet/e (bitte ankreuzen):
I am interested in (please mark with a cross):

:.... Architektur | Architecture

:.... Malerei | Painting

:.... Design | Design

:.... Kunsthandwerk allgemein | Arts and Crafts

:.... Schmuck | Jewelry

:.... Metall | Metal

:.... Glas | Glass

:.... Keramik | Ceramics

:.... Textile Kunst | Textile Art

Ich möchte den Vorteil der preisgünstigen Subskription
nutzen und bitte Sie, mich vor dem Erscheinen neuer
MARKENLEXIKA unverbindlich zu informieren:

I want to take advantage of cheaper subscription prices.
Please send me information on new ENCYCLOPEDIAS OF
MARKS before their publication, with no obligation to buy:

:.... GLAS-MARKENLEXIKON 1600–1945
Signaturen, Fabrik- und Handelsmarken
Europa und Nordamerika
ISBN 3-925369-37-6
Subskriptionspreis DM 348,– (später DM 398,–)

:.... GLAS-MARKENLEXIKON 1600–1945
CD-ROM mit Begleitheft
ISBN 3-925369-39-2
DM 598,–

:.... METALL-MARKENLEXIKON, 1881–1945
Metalle – Schmuck, Bestecke, edle und unedle Objekte
Deutschland

:.... KERAMIK-MARKENLEXIKON 1945–1995
Porzellan und Keramik Report
Europa (Festland)

Antwort | Reply

ARNOLDSCHE

Verlagsanstalt GmbH

Senefelderstr. 8

D-70178 Stuttgart

Absender | Sender

Name/Vorname

....

Straße/Hausnummer

....

Land/PLZ/Ort

....

Gerne informieren wir auch Freunde und Bekannte von Ihnen über unsere Reihe „Architektur, Kunst, Kunsthandwerk und Design vom 16. bis 20. Jh."; tragen Sie einfach unten die entsprechende Adresse ein.

Please provide the names and addresses of interested friends and acquaintances. We will be glad to keep them informed about our publications in the „Architecture, Art, Applied Art and Design from the 16th through the 20th Century" series.

Empfehlung | Recommendation

Name/Vorname

....

Straße/Hausnummer

....

Land/PLZ/Ort

Georges Fouquet

Kollier »Fuchsie«
Gold, Opale, Diamanten, Perlen, Email
um 1905
Höhe ca. 15 cm
Musée du Petit Palais, Paris

Necklace "Fuchsia"
Gold, opals, diamonds, pearls, enamel
ca 1905
Height approx 15 cm
Musée du Petit Palais, Paris

Georges Fouquet

Anhänger »Calla«
Gold, Diamanten, Opale, Email,
Perle
um 1900
Breite 4,7 cm
Hessisches Landesmuseum,
Darmstadt

Pendant "Calla lily"
Gold, diamonds, opals, enamel,
pearl
ca 1900
Width 4.7 cm
Hessisches Landesmuseum,
Darmstadt

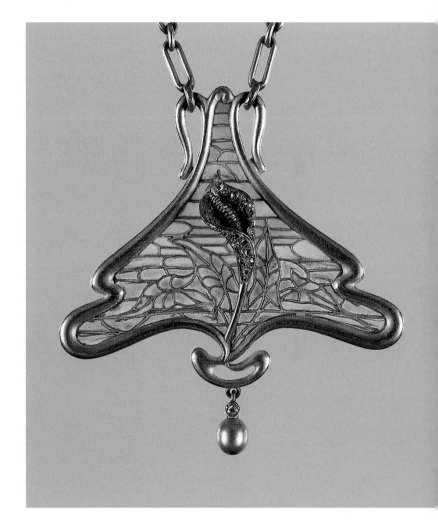

Georges Fouquet

Anhänger »Glyzinie«
Gold, Email, Perlen
um 1908/10
Länge 10,8 cm
Rijksmuseum, Amsterdam

Pendant "Wistaria"
Gold, enamel, pearls
ca 1908/10
Length 10.8 cm
Rijksmuseum, Amsterdam

Georges Fouquet

Anhänger »Kornblumen«
in Anlehnung an einen Entwurf
von Alphonse Mucha
Gold, Diamanten, Perlen, Email
um 1907/08
Breite 5,3 cm
Musée du Petit Palais, Paris

Pendant "Cornflowers"
after a design by Alphonse Mucha
Gold, diamonds, pearls, enamel
ca 1907/08
Width 5.3 cm
Musée du Petit Palais, Paris

Georges Fouquet

Brosche »Landschaft«
Gold, Email, Perlen
Fensteremailplatte wohl von
Etienne Tourette
um 1904/05
Breite 6,4 cm
Schmuckmuseum Pforzheim
(Dauerleihgabe des Landes
Baden-Württemberg)

Brooch "Landscape"
Gold, enamel, pearls
Email à jour plaque probably by
Etienne Tourette
ca 1904/05
Width 6.4 cm
Schmuckmuseum Pforzheim
(on permanent loan from the State
of Baden-Württemberg)

Georges Fouquet

Haarstecker »Nelken«
Entwurf von Charles Desrosiers
Horn, Gold, Diamanten, Email
1906
Höhe 15,5 cm
Musée des Arts Décoratifs, Paris

Hairpin "Carnations"
Design Charles Desrosiers
Horn, gold, diamonds, enamel
1906
Height 15.5 cm
Musée des Arts Décoratifs, Paris

Léopold Gautrait

Léopold Gautrait

Man kennt ihn nicht, den *Ziseleur-Modelleur* und *treuen Mitarbeiter* in der Firma des Léon Gariod in Paris, man weiß nichts über seine Herkunft, sein Leben, seine Ausbildung und seinen Charakter. Man kennt lediglich einige Schmuckstücke, die die gestempelte Signatur *L. Gautrait* und meistens auch die Firmenmarke von Léon Gariod tragen. Es ist bekannt, daß manches mit der Gautrait-Signatur bezeichnete Schmuckstück bei berühmten Pariser Juwelieren verkauft (auch hergestellt?) wurde, wie zum Beispiel der *Pfauenanhänger,* den im Jahre 1900 ein Pforzheimer Geschäftsmann im Hause Vever erworben hat. Wir kennen Gautrait ausschließlich von seinem Œuvre, das dem allgemeinen Formenkanon und Repertoire des Art Nouveau-Schmucks verpflichtet ist, allerdings auf sehr hohem, die ornamentale Kraft der Linien und die Dreidimensionalität höchst wirkungsvoll nutzendem, künstlerisch anspruchsvollem Niveau.

Gautraits Auswahl der Motive ist breit gefächert. Er liebt die Tiere, im besonderen die Vögel: den Parade-Vogel des Jugendstils, den Pfau ebenso wie die Schwalbe, auch die sonst eher seltene Eule, und es gibt bei einem erst kürzlich bekanntgewordenen Anhänger eine Spinne. Nicht grundsätzlich und doch auffallend häufig steht die Tiergestalt in einem Landschaftsausschnitt – die Schwalbe fliegt über einen Blütenzweig, der Uhu sitzt vor einer Baumkulisse auf einem Ast, die Spinne hat ihr zartes Netz zwischen zwei Farnwedel gespannt.

Wie manch anderer Schmuckkünstler seiner Zeit befaßte sich Gautrait mit fabelhaften Mischwesen: eine *Fledermausfrau* – die weibliche Büste mit den durchscheinenden Flügeln des geheimnisvollen Nachttieres deutet Phantastisch-Symbolisches an –, ein Anhänger als geflügeltes Fabelwesen ist gleichzeitig eine ägyptische Gottheit, Vogel und schlangenartiges Reptil. Gautraits *Frauenbüste*-Anhänger beweist wie seine Tierdarstellungen und die gelegentlichen Blüten-Schmuckstücke ein hohes Maß an Kreativität in der Umsetzung der Naturform in das fließende Ornament des Jugendstils.

Bemerkenswert ist, daß sich Gautrait kurz nach 1900 vom Art Nouveau abwendet: Broschen, Armbänder und Colliers, die auch in der Zusammenarbeit mit Gariod entstanden, sind in verblüffendem Maße einem Neoklassizismus verpflichtet, der keine Erinnerungen an den Jugendstil mehr zuläßt.

Signatur von Léopold Gautrait auf einem Schmuckstück, um 1900

Léopold Gautrait's signature on a piece of jewellery, ca 1900

Léopold Gautrait

All that is known about Léopold Gautrait is that he was a *ciseleur-modeleur* and *loyal employee* at the Paris firm of Léon Gariod. Nothing is known of his origins, his biography, the training he underwent or even his personality. A few pieces of jewellery bearing the stamped signature *L. Gautrait* and the Léon Gautrait mark are his legacy. Some pieces of his were sold (perhaps also made?) by reputable Paris jewellers. One of these is the *peacock pendant* bought in 1900 from Maison Vever by a Pforzheim businessman. We know Gautrait solely through his work, which reveals his commitment to the formal canon and repertoire of Art Nouveau. The Gautrait pieces are, however, of an exceptionally high standard. Their creator knew how to combine decorative line with plasticity to maximum effect.

Gautrait's range of motifs includes animals and birds, which seem to have been his favourites – the Art Nouveau emblem, the peacock, as well as the swallow and even the owl, which is rare among Art Nouveau motifs. A Gautrait spider pendant has recently come to light. His animal motifs are often set in a landscape detail. A swallow is flying over a flowering branch; an owl is perched on a branch against a backdrop of trees and the spider has spun its delicate web between two fern fronds.

Like so many of his contemporaries, Gautrait was obviously fascinated by mythical beings. A *bat lady* (the bust of a woman with the translucent wings of the nocturnal creature) is an intimation of fantastic Symbolism. A pendant in the form of a winged mythical being is an Egyptian deity, a bird and a serpent-like reptile in one. Gautrait's *female busts* as pendants and his animal and flower motifs represent highly imaginative translation of natural shapes into fluid Art Nouveau ornaments.

Oddly, Gautrait abandoned Art Nouveau shortly after 1900. The brooches, bracelets and chokers he made for Gariod are noticeably Neo-Classical in style.

Léopold Gautrait

Anhänger »Farn und Spinne«
Gold, Topase, Peridot, Email
um 1898
Breite 7,3 cm
Schmuckmuseum Pforzheim
(Werner Wild-Stiftung)

Pendant "Fern and spider"
Gold, topazes, peridot, enamel
ca 1898
Width 7.3 cm
Schmuckmuseum Pforzheim
(Werner Wild-Stiftung)

Léopold Gautrait

Anhänger »Fledermausfrau«
Entwurf Gautrait, Ausführung
Gariod
Gold, Email, Perle
um 1900
Breite 3 cm
Badisches Landesmuseum, Karlsruhe

Pendant "Bat Lady"
Design Gautrait, execution Gariod
Gold, enamel, pearl
ca 1900
Width 3 cm
Badisches Landesmuseum, Karlsruhe

Léopold Gautrait

Anhänger »Frauenbüste«
Gold, Diamanten, Smaragde,
Topas, Email, Perle
um 1900
Breite 4,6 cm
Hessisches Landesmuseum,
Darmstadt

Pendant "Bust of a woman"
Gold, diamonds, emeralds, topaz,
enamel, pearl
ca 1900
Width 4.6 cm
Hessisches Landesmuseum,
Darmstadt

Léopold Gautrait

Anhänger an Kette
»Geflügeltes Fabelwesen«
Gold, Diamanten, Smaragd,
Email, Perle
um 1900
Breite 4,5 cm
Bayerisches Nationalmuseum,
München

Pendant on chain
"Winged mythical being"
Gold, diamonds, emerald,
enamel, pearl
ca 1900
Width 4.5 cm
Bayerisches Nationalmuseum,
Munich

Léopold Gautrait

Anhänger »Schwalbe«
Gold, Diamant, Email, Perlen
um 1899/1900
Breite 5,4 cm
Museum Schwäbisch Gmünd

Pendant "Swallow"
Gold, diamond, enamel, pearls
ca 1899/1900
Width 5.4 cm
Museum Schwäbisch Gmünd

Léopold Gautrait

Anhänger/Brosche »Pfau«
Gold, Opale, Diamanten,
Smaragde, Email
um 1899/1900
Breite 7 cm
Schmuckmuseum Pforzheim

Pendant/brooch "Peacock"
Gold, opals, diamonds, emeralds,
enamel
ca 1899/1900
Width 7 cm
Schmuckmuseum Pforzheim

Léopold Gautrait

Anhänger »Nelke«
Gold, Diamanten, Email, Perle
um 1904
Breite 4,5 cm
Slg. Dr. Brigitte Marquardt

Pendant "Carnation"
Gold, diamonds, enamel, pearl
ca 1904
Width 4.5 cm
Dr. Brigitte Marquardt Collection

Lucien Gaillard

Lucien Gaillard

Firmeninserat, um 1901
Firm advertisement, ca 1901

Wie kein anderer Künstler in der Welt des Jugendstilschmucks beschäftigte sich Lucien Gaillard mit der Kunst Japans, die seit den 70er Jahren des 19. Jahrhunderts größte Beachtung und Bewunderung in Europa fand. Nachdem er, der als Silberschmied in der Firma seines Vaters ausgebildet worden war, sich intensiv mit den formalen und handwerklich-technischen Qualitäten der japanischen Kunst und des Kunsthandwerks auseinandergesetzt hatte und sich nach der Weltausstellung von 1900 und unter dem Eindruck der dort von René Lalique präsentierten Arbeiten mehr und mehr der Gestaltung von Schmuckstücken widmete, avancierte Lucien Gaillard sehr schnell zu einem der führenden Schmuckkünstler des Art Nouveau. Trotz aller selbst erworbenen Fertigkeiten reichten ihm die Kenntnisse der traditionellen Handwerkstechniken nicht aus. Er verpflichtete deshalb japanische Kunsthandwerker – ähnlich wie dies auf anderen Gebieten künstlerischen Schaffens im Art Nouveau-Zentrum Nancy geschah –, um seine eigenen Vorstellungen in seiner Pariser Werkstätte bestmöglich verwirklichen zu können.

Auf diese Weise entstanden Schmuckstücke, vornehmlich Zierkämme und Haarstecker (in Japan gehörten die *Kushi*, *Kanzashi* und *Kogai* seit Jahrhunderten zum Schmuckrepertoire der vornehmen Frau und der Geisha), die die Anregungen aus Japan aufnahmen und wohl gerade deshalb zu den überzeugendsten Schöpfungen der französischen Schmuckkunst des Art Nouveau gehören.

Es ist daher nicht verwunderlich, daß zarte Blütenkompositionen – Apfelblüten, Flieder, Schafgarbe- und Holunderblütenstände – im Werk Gaillards so häufig zu finden sind. Naheliegend ist auch, daß er, wie schon zuvor sein großes Vorbild Lalique, dem Horn in äußerst delikater Behandlung durch zurückhaltende Patinierung und durch kunstvolle Schnitz- und Graviertechniken einen hohen Stellenwert einräumte, gehörten doch Horn und Schildpatt zu den bevorzugten Materialien des von ihm so bewunderten traditionellen Haarschmucks im alten Japan. Lucien Gaillard war ein brillanter Vermittler zwischen Ostasien und dem Paris der Jahrhundertwende.

Rekisentei Yeiri
Die Kurtisane Morokoshi mit
Haarschmuck, um 1795

Rekisentei Yeiri
The courtisan Morokoshi wearing
hair ornaments, ca 1795

Lucien Gaillard

Lucien Gaillard was the Art Nouveau jewellery designer and jeweller most familiar with Japanese art, which swept Europe from the 1870s. After training as a silversmith in his father's firm Gaillard went deeply into the Japanese fine and applied arts, learning as much as he could both formally and technically. Greatly impressed by René Lalique's jewellery shown at the 1900 Paris Exhibition, Lucien Gaillard became increasingly committed to innovative jewellery design. However, Japanese artisans were already working in Nancy, a stronghold of Art Nouveau. Not content with demonstrating his skill in the traditional European techniques of his craft, Gaillard turned to Japanese craftsmen to implement his ideas at his Paris atelier.

Gaillard's association with Japanese artisans led to the creation of decorative pieces, primarily combs and hairpins (in Japan *Kushi, Kanzashi* and *Kogai* had been worn by elegant ladies and geishas for centuries). Japanese aesthetic currents and jewellery-making techniques were thus taken up and transformed into some of the most compelling creations in French Art Nouveau jewellery.

Delicate floral compositions featuring apple blossom, lilac, yarrow and elder flower motifs figure prominently in Gaillard's jewellery. Like Lalique, who had originally inspired him, Gaillard prized horn as a material for jewellery, subjecting it to sophisticated treatment, including subtle patination and innovative carving and engraving techniques. Horn and tortoiseshell are, after all, the materials traditionally used for making

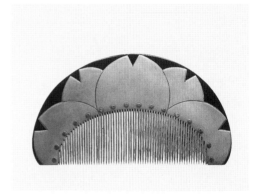

Japanische Zierkämme, Mitte 19. Jahrhundert

Japanese ornamental combs, mid-19th century

hair ornaments in Japan. Lucien Gaillard was the brilliant mediator between East Asia and Fin de Siècle Paris.

Lucien Gaillard

Haarstecker »Schafgarbe«
Horn, Gold, Diamanten
um 1903
Breite 11 cm
Schmuckmuseum Pforzheim

Hairpin "Yarrow"
Horn, gold, diamonds
ca 1903
Width 11 cm
Schmuckmuseum Pforzheim

Lucien Gaillard

Haarstecker »Ahornfrüchte«
Horn, Silber
zwischen 1902 und 1906
Höhe 12,9 cm
Rijksmuseum, Amsterdam

Hairpin "Maple seeds"
Horn, silver
between 1902 and 1906
Height 12.9 cm
Rijksmuseum, Amsterdam

Lucien Gaillard

Haarstecker »Holunder«
Horn, Gold, Perlen
zwischen 1900 und 1905
Breite 10,8 cm
MAK – Österreichisches Museum
für angewandte Kunst, Wien

Hairpin "Elder flower"
Horn, gold, pearls
between 1900 and 1905
Width 10.8 cm
MAK – Österreichisches Museum
für angewandte Kunst, Vienna

Lucien Gaillard

Haarstecker »Hortensie«
Horn, Gold, Rubine
zwischen 1902 und 1905
Höhe 14 cm
Bayerisches Nationalmuseum,
München

Hairpin "Hydrangea"
Horn, gold, rubies
between 1902 and 1905
Height 14 cm
Bayerisches Nationalmuseum,
Munich

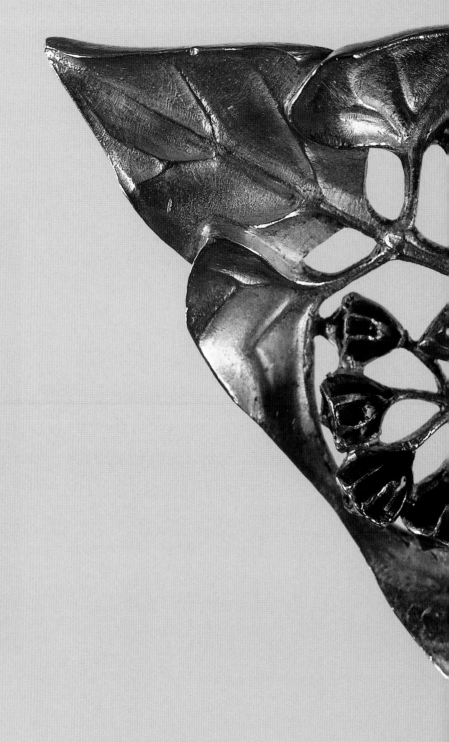

Lucien Gaillard

Brosche »Efeu«
Gold, Amethyst, Email
um 1900
Breite 5 cm
Hessisches Landesmuseum,
Darmstadt

Brooch "Ivy"
Gold, amethyst, enamel
ca 1900
Width 5 cm
Hessisches Landesmuseum,
Darmstadt

Lucien Gaillard

Haarspange »Apfelblüten«
Horn, Gold, Rubine
um 1903/04
Breite 9 cm
Schmuckmuseum Pforzheim

Hair-slide "Apple blossoms"
Horn, gold, rubies
ca 1903/04
Width 9 cm
Schmuckmuseum Pforzheim

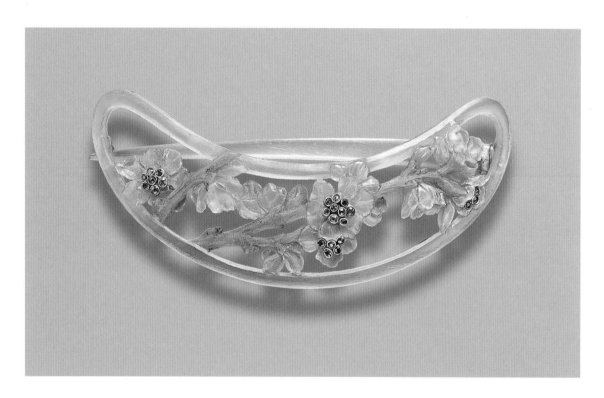

Lucien Gaillard

Schmuckkamm »Flieder«
Horn, Gold, Diamanten
zwischen 1900 und 1905
Höhe 17,6 cm
MAK – Österreichisches Museum
für angewandte Kunst, Wien

Ornamental comb "Lilac"
Horn, gold, diamonds
between 1900 and 1905
Height 17.6 cm
MAK – Österreichisches Museum
für angewandte Kunst, Vienna

Lucien Gaillard

Anhänger »Käfer«
Silber patiniert, Peridot, Email
nach 1900
Länge 9 cm
Hessisches Landesmuseum,
Darmstadt

Pendant "Beetle"
Silver, patinated, peridot, enamel
after 1900
Length 9 cm
Hessisches Landesmuseum,
Darmstadt

Lucien Gaillard

Schließe »Ahornfrüchte«
Horn, Silber
zwischen 1900 und 1905
Breite 8,4 cm
MAK – Österreichisches Museum
für angewandte Kunst, Wien

Buckle "Maple seeds"
Horn, silver
between 1900 and 1905
Width 8.4 cm
MAK – Österreichisches Museum
für angewandte Kunst, Vienna

Lucien Gaillard

Collier-de-chien-Platte
»Geißblattblüten«
Horn, Gold, Diamanten
um 1900
Breite 10 cm
Badisches Landesmuseum, Karlsruhe
Abb. S. 76/77

Collier-de-chien-clasp "Woodbines"
Horn, gold, diamonds
ca 1900
Width 10 cm
Badisches Landesmuseum, Karlsruhe
ill. p. 76/77

Lucien Gaillard

Ring »Uhu«
Gold, Email
zwischen 1900 und 1905
Durchmesser 2 cm
MAK – Österreichisches Museum
für angewandte Kunst, Wien

Ring "Owl"
Gold, enamel
between 1900 and 1905
Diameter 2 cm
MAK – Österreichisches Museum
für angewandte Kunst, Vienna

Lucien Gaillard

Ring »Stiefmütterchen«
Gold, Email
um 1900
Länge des Ringkopfes 3,8 cm
Schmuckmuseum Pforzheim

Ring "Pansies"
Gold, enamel
ca 1900
Length of bezel 3.8 cm
Schmuckmuseum Pforzheim

Henri Vever

Die Maison Vever

Titelgestaltung (Detail) des Buches
»La Bijouterie Française au XIXᵉ Siècle«
von Henri Vever, Paris 1908

Cover (detail) of the book "La Bijouterie
Française au XIXᵉ Siècle" by Henri Vever,
Paris 1908

Lang ist die Tradition des Hauses Vever, von den Anfängen im lothringischen Metz bis zu den großen Erfolgen, die die Enkel des Firmengründers, Paul und Henri Vever, im Paris der Belle Époque feiern konnten. Wie für viele andere brachte im Jahre 1900 die *Exposition Universelle* auch für die Maison Vever, für die der junge Lalique in den 80er Jahren eine kurze Zeit gearbeitet hatte, einen Höhepunkt in ihrer Geschichte.

War das Haus über Jahrzehnte eher der konventionellen Juweliertradition verpflichtet, so veränderten die den neuen Ideen aufgeschlossenen *Vever Frères* nach der Übernahme 1881 den Stil der Firma. Beide waren handwerklich und wohl auch künstlerisch versiert, der überzeugende Erfolg im Sinne der Art Nouveau-Schmuckkunst resultierte aber vornehmlich aus der engen und kontinuierlichen Zusammenarbeit mit renommierten Künstlern und »Designern« der damaligen Zeit.

Es ist bekannt, daß Léopold Gautrait für Vever gearbeitet hat, auch Georges Le Turcq, vermutlich der Emailleur Etienne Tourette und mancher andere. Ausschlaggebend für das hohe Ansehen der Maison Vever war jedoch die langanhaltende Kooperation mit Eugène Grasset, von dem ein Großteil der Entwürfe stammt, mit denen Vever auf der Weltausstellung von 1900 neben Lalique und Fouquet im Mittelpunkt des Interesses stand.

Grasset wurde 1841 in Lausanne geboren, seit 1871 lebte er in Paris. Auf nahezu allen Gebieten der angewandten Kunst war er – der ursprünglich Architektur studiert hatte – als Entwerfer tätig. Er war auch Buchillu-strator und Maler, seine besondere Liebe und Aufmerksamkeit galt der japanischen Kunst. Die von Grasset für Vever entworfenen Schmuckstücke spielten das ganze Repertoire des Art Nouveau durch: Mischwesen und Insektenfrauen wie die berühmte *Sylvia,* Vögel wie Pfauen, Schwalben und Schwäne, Blüten und Pflanzen, auch literarische Motive gehören zum thematischen Umfeld, in dem sich Eugène Grasset als Schmuckentwerfer bewegte.

Andere Arbeiten aus dem Hause Vever machen deutlich, wie dominierend die Stellung René Laliques war. Manches Schmuckstück mit der Signatur VEVER ist an ein Vorbild angelehnt, das als Erfindung des Hauptmeisters der Art Nouveau-Schmuckkunst zur Nachempfindung reizte. Keinesfalls aber ist durch diese Tatsache der hohe Rang des Hauses Vever beeinträchtigt.

La Maison Vever

Vever is a venerable institution. Founded in Metz, Lorraine, Maison Vever flourished in the Belle Époque under the founder's grandsons, Paul and Henri Vever. The young Lalique had worked briefly for Vever in the 1880s. The 1900 Paris Exhibition represented, as for so many other Art Nouveau designers and jewellers, the pinnacle of success crowning a long career.

Before 1881, *Maison Vever* had worked on more or less conventional lines until the firm became Vever Frères, changing its style with its name and becoming responsive to new ideas. Both brothers were accomplished craftsmen and designers. Their new Art Nouveau jewellery owed its popularity largely to close collaboration with the most famous artists and designers of the period.

Léopold Gautrait worked for Vever and so did Georges Le Turcq, the enameller Étienne Tourette and many other illustrious contemporaries. However, what made the reputation of Maison Vever was collaboration with Eugène Grasset over a long period of time. He designed most of the pieces with which Vever, like Lalique and Fouquet, attracted so much attention at the 1900 Paris Exhibition.

Born in Lausanne on Lake Geneva in 1841, Grasset lived in Paris from 1871. Although he had originally trained as an architect, Grasset worked in all fields of the decorative and applied arts. He was active as a book illustrator and painter, with a strong bias towards Japanese art. The jewellery Grasset designed for Vever brought the full gamut of Art Nouveau motifs and design into play. His thematic range encompassed mythical monsters and insect ladies like his famous *Sylvia,* peacocks, swallows and swans, flowers, plants and even literary motifs. As a jewellery designer Eugène Grasset was one of the most versatile of his day.

Much of the jewellery sold by Maison Vever bears eloquent witness to the dominant status of René Lalique. Many pieces bearing the VEVER signature were modelled on designs by Lalique. The leading protagonist of Art Nouveau jewellery design stimulated the inventiveness of his contemporaries. The fact that Lalique was copied within the firm does not, however, detract from the deservedly high repute of Maison Vever.

Signatur auf einem Schmuckstück, um 1900

Signature on a piece of jewellery, ca 1900

Henri Vever

Hutnadel »Tänzerin«
Entwurf von Georges Le Turcq
Gold
um 1900/01
Höhe der Figur 5,6 cm
Schmuckmuseum Pforzheim

Hatpin "Ballerina"
Design Georges Le Turcq
Gold
ca 1900/01
Height of figure 5.6 cm
Schmuckmuseum Pforzheim

Henri Vever

Anhänger »Le Réveil«
Gold, Elfenbein, Diamant, Email
1900
Länge 9,5 cm
Musée des Arts Décoratifs, Paris

Pendant "Le Réveil"
Gold, ivory, diamond, enamel
1900
Length 9.5 cm
Musée des Arts Décoratifs, Paris

Henri Vever

Anhänger »Irisfrau«
Gold, Topas, Diamanten, Perle,
Email
1900
Länge 6,3 cm
Musée des Arts Décoratifs, Paris

Pendant "Iris Lady"
Gold, topaz, diamonds, pearl,
enamel
1900
Length 6.3 cm
Musée des Arts Décoratifs, Paris

Henri Vever

Anhänger »Poésie«
Entwurf von Eugène Grasset
Gold, Elfenbein, Email
1900
Länge 11,2 cm
Musée des Arts Décoratifs, Paris

Pendant "Poésie"
Design Eugène Grasset
Gold, ivory, enamel
1900
Length 11.2 cm
Musée des Arts Décoratifs, Paris

Henri Vever

Anhänger »La Sève«
Gold, Rubin, Peridot, Amethyst,
Smaragd, Topas, Kunzit, Perle,
Email
um 1900/01
Länge 9,3 cm
Schmuckmuseum Pforzheim

Pendant "La Sève"
Gold, ruby, peridot, amethyst,
emerald, topaz, kunzit, pearl, enamel
ca 1900/01
Length 9.3 cm
Schmuckmuseum Pforzheim

Henri Vever

Anhänger »Le Parfum«
Gold, Opal, Perle, Email
1900
Länge 7 cm
Musée des Arts Décoratifs, Paris

Pendant "Le Parfum"
Gold, opal, pearl, enamel
1900
Length 7 cm
Musée des Arts Décoratifs, Paris

Henri Vever

Schmuckkamm »Mistelzweig«
Horn, Gold, Perlen
um 1899
Höhe 16,1 cm
Museum für Kunst und Gewerbe,
Hamburg

Ornamental comb "Mistletoe"
Horn, gold, pearls
ca 1899
Height 16.1 cm
Museum für Kunst und Gewerbe,
Hamburg

Henri Vever

Schmuckkamm »Algenornament«
Horn, Gold, Amethyste, Email
um 1900/02
Höhe 17 cm
Privatbesitz

Ornamental comb "Algae"
Horn, gold, amethysts, enamel
ca 1900/02
Height 17 cm
Private collection

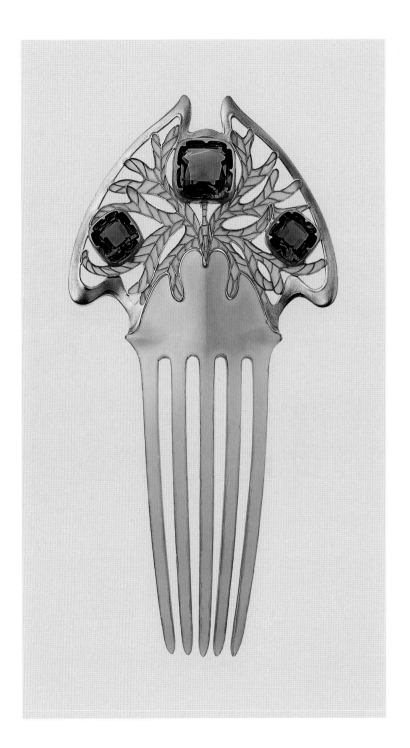

Henri Vever

Schmuckkamm »Schwäne und
Seerosen«
Entwurf von Eugène Grasset
Horn, Gold, Elfenbein, Email
um 1900
Höhe 15 cm
Musée du Petit Palais, Paris

Ornamental comb "Swans and
water-lilies"
Design Eugène Grasset
Horn, gold, ivory, enamel
ca 1900
Height 15 cm
Musée du Petit Palais, Paris

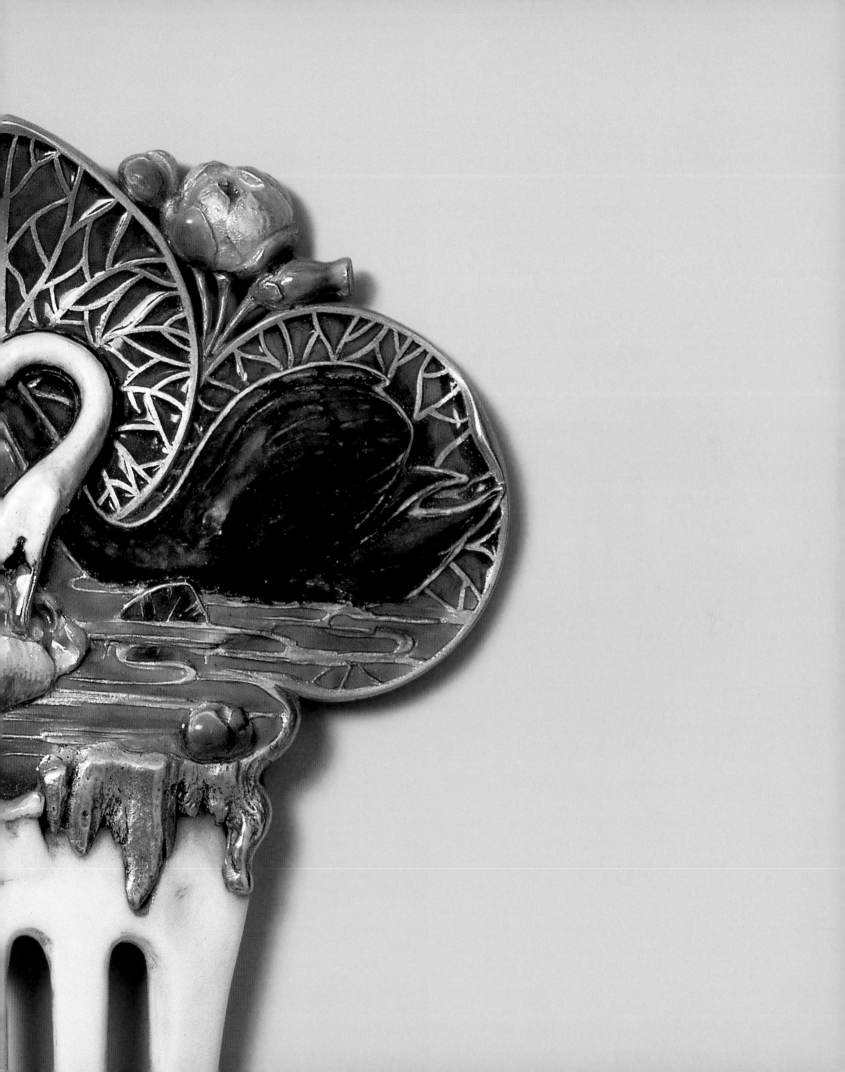

Henri Vever

Gürtelschließe »Pfau«
Entwurf von Eugène Grasset
Gold, Karneol, Email
1900
Breite 6,5 cm
Musée des Arts Décoratifs, Paris

Belt buckle "Peacock"
Design Eugène Grasset
Gold, cornelian, enamel
1900
Width 6.5 cm
Musée des Arts Décoratifs, Paris

Henri Vever

Gürtelschließe »Zwei Störe«
Entwurf von Eugène Grasset
Gold, Rubine, Peridote, Email
1899/1900
Höhe 9,2 cm
Württembergisches Landes-
museum, Stuttgart

Belt buckle "Two sturgeons"
Design Eugène Grasset
Gold, rubies, peridots, enamel
1899/1900
Height 9.2 cm
Württembergisches Landesmuseum,
Stuttgart

Henri Vever

Anhänger »Sylvia«
Gold, Achat, Diamanten, Rubine,
Email
um 1900
Länge 12 cm
Musée des Arts Décoratifs, Paris

Pendant "Sylvia"
Gold, agate, diamonds, rubies,
enamel
ca 1900
Length 12 cm
Musée des Arts Décoratifs, Paris

Henri Vever

Anhänger »Femme aux Tambourins«
Gold, Perle, Email
1900
Länge 7,5 cm
Musée des Arts Décoratifs, Paris

Pendant "Femme aux Tambourins"
Gold, pearl, enamel
1900
Length 7.5 cm
Musée des Arts Décoratifs, Paris

Henri Vever

Anhänger »Glyzinie«
Entwurf wohl von Georges Le Turcq
Gold, Opale, Diamanten, Email
um 1900
Länge 11 cm
Schmuckmuseum Pforzheim

Pendant "Wisteria"
Design probably Georges Le Turcq
Gold, opals, diamonds, enamel
ca 1900
Length 11 cm
Schmuckmuseum Pforzheim

Philippe Wolfers

Philippe Wolfers

Philippe Wolfers, um/ca 1905

An der Pariser Weltausstellung des Jahres 1900 nahm Philippe Wolfers nicht teil, obwohl es dort eine belgische Sektion gab. Sein Auftritt in Paris fand im Rahmen einer Einzelausstellung in der privaten Galerie Aublanc statt.

Seit 1892 war Philippe der künstlerische Leiter der bis zu fünfzig Mitarbeiter beschäftigenden Gold- und Silbermanufaktur *Wolfers Frères* in Brüssel, die er zusammen mit seinen Brüdern Max und Robert führte. Der wie so viele Künstler des Jugendstils an der Kunst Japans interessierte Philippe war nicht nur deshalb sehr empfänglich für die Ideen und Formen des Art Nouveau, die er zumindest anfänglich symptomatisch verband mit der historistischen Tradition, die im Hause Wolfers jahrzehntelang gepflegt worden war. Ein überzeugendes Beispiel

hierfür ist der Anhänger *Paon Renaissance* (siehe Seite 103), der japanisches Formgefühl mit europäisch-historisierenden Ornamenten zu einem Schmuckstück von eigenartigem Reiz verbindet.

Philippe Wolfers zeichnerisches Talent drückte sich in zahllosen Naturstudien aus: Insekten, Vögel, im besonderen Pflanzen unterschiedlichster Art fanden sein Interesse. Anfänglich ganz naturalistisch, dann abstrahiert und ornamental verwandelt entstanden somit gleichsam Vorlagen für die Schmuckstücke, die Wolfers – außerhalb und unabhängig von den Produkten der großen Manufaktur – als numerierte Unikate *(exemplaires uniques)* schuf. Sein ausgeprägtes Gefühl für plastische Werte – der junge Philippe hatte neben Zeichnen auch Kurse für Bildhauerei belegt und pflegte dies sein Leben lang – trug dazu bei, daß dieser Unikatschmuck sowohl formal-ornamental als auch in der Dreidimensionalität hohen künstlerischen Ansprüchen genügte.

Obwohl ohne den französischen Art Nouveau nicht denkbar, hat der Schmuck von Philippe Wolfers seinen ganz eigenen Charakter. Nicht so gefällig fließend wie viele Pariser Stücke sind die Schmuckstücke des Belgiers eher herb, manche sogar fast düster oder geradezu bedrohlich. Wolfers, der mit Sicherheit Laliques Œuvre kannte – über eine persönliche Begegnung gibt es unterschiedliche Aussagen –, hat als individueller Künstler seinen eigenen Art Nouveau-Ausdruck gefunden in einer Stadt, die nicht nur durch Architekten wie Paul Hankar und Victor Horta zu einem eigenständigen Jugendstilzentrum geworden war.

Die Ehefrau von Philippe Wolfers mit der Gürtelschließe »Orchideen«, 1897

Philippe Wolfers' wife wearing "Orchids", a belt buckle he designed, 1897

Philippe Wolfers

Philippe Wolfers was one Art Nouveau jewellery designer who did not show work at the 1900 Paris Exhibition although it had a Belgian section. A one-man show at the Aublanc Gallery was Wolfers' stepping-stone to success in Paris.

From 1892 Philippe Wolfers was design director for *Wolfers Frères,* jewellers and goldsmiths in Brussels. He had up to fifty artisans working under him and shared the management of the firm with his brothers Max and Robert. Like so many of his contemporaries, Philippe Wolfers was fascinated by Japanese art. At first committed to the historicizing tradition which the firm of Wolfers had followed for decades, Philippe Wolfers embraced the ideas and forms of Art Nouveau enthusiastically. A striking example of this mixed allegiance is the pendant *Renaissance Peacock* (see page 103), which combines a Japanese feeling for form with the decorative bent of European Historicism. For all its eclecticism, this is a stunning and highly unusual piece of jewellery.

Philippe Wolfers' talents as a draughtsman found expression in studies from nature. Insects, birds and rare plants of all kinds intrigued him. At first he designed in an entirely naturalistic style, later abandoning it to work with abstract forms, which he translated into ornamental shapes. Wolfers also drew the studies for jewellery which he made into one-of-a-kind creations *(exemplaires uniques).* Philippe Wolfers had taken courses in sculpture as well as drawing in his youth and he never lost touch with the third dimension. Consequently, his one-of-a-kind pieces are of a consistently high standard and distin-

guished by an added touch of aesthetically satisfying plasticity.

Although indebted to French Art Nouveau, Philippe Wolfers went his own way. Less sinuously fluid than that of some Paris contemporaries, the Belgian designer's work tends to astringency and some of it seems bleak-looking, if not positively ominous. Wolfers was presumably well acquainted with Lalique's work (accounts differ on whether the two actually met). Be that as it may, Philippe Wolfers succeeded in finding his own distinctive Art Nouveau form of expression in a city which is a byword for Art Nouveau as a total work of art, the creation of versatile architects like Paul Hankar and Victor Horta.

Philippe Wolfers in seinem Atelier, um 1905

Philippe Wolfers in his atelier, ca 1905

Philippe Wolfers

Anhänger »Orchidée ailée«
Gold, Opal, Diamanten, Rubine,
Perle, Email
1902
Breite 5,7 cm
Privatbesitz Amsterdam

Pendant "Orchidée ailée"
Gold, opal, diamonds, rubies, pearl,
enamel
1902
Width 5.7 cm
Private collection, Amsterdam

Philippe Wolfers

Anhänger/Brosche
»Grande Libellule«
Gold, Opale, Rubine, Diamanten,
Email
1903/04
Breite 13 cm
A.S.B.L. Philippe et Marcel Wolfers,
Brüssel

Pendant/brooch "Grande Libellule"
Gold, opals, rubies, diamonds,
enamel
1903/04
Width 13 cm
A.S.B.L. Philippe et Marcel Wolfers,
Brussels

Philippe Wolfers

Anhänger »Schwan«
Gold, Diamanten, Rubine, Perle,
Email
um 1900
Länge 7 cm
Schmuckmuseum Pforzheim

Pendant "Swan"
Gold, diamonds, rubies, pearl, ena-
mel
ca 1900
Length 7 cm
Schmuckmuseum Pforzheim

Philippe Wolfers

Anhänger »Paon Renaissance«
Gold, Smaragde, Perlen, Email
um 1901/02
Länge 15,5 cm
Privatbesitz Brüssel

Pendant "Paon Renaissance"
Gold, emeralds, pearls, enamel
ca 1901/02
Length 15.5 cm
Private collection, Brussels

Philippe Wolfers

Anhänger/Brosche »Nike«
Gold, Rubine, Diamanten,
Turmalin, Karneol, Perle, Email
1902
Breite 7 cm
A.S.B.L. Philippe et Marcel Wolfers,
Brüssel

Pendant/brooch "Nike"
Gold, rubies, diamonds, tourmaline,
cornelian, pearl, enamel
1902
Width 7 cm
A.S.B.L. Philippe et Marcel Wolfers,
Brussels

Philippe Wolfers

Anhänger »Cygne et deux Serpents«
Gold, Opal, Diamanten, Rubine,
Perle
1899
Breite 5 cm
A.S.B.L. Philippe et Marcel Wolfers,
Brüssel

Pendant "Swan and two serpents"
Gold, opal, diamonds, rubies, pearl
1899
Width 5 cm
A.S.B.L. Philippe et Marcel Wolfers,
Brussels

Philippe Wolfers

Gürtelschließe »Plume et Paon«
Gold, Diamant, Opale, Rubine
1898
Breite 7 cm
A.S.B.L. Philippe et Marcel Wolfers,
Brüssel

Belt buckle "Plume et Paon"
Gold, diamond, opals, rubies
1898
Width 7 cm
A.S.B.L. Philippe et Marcel Wolfers,
Brussels

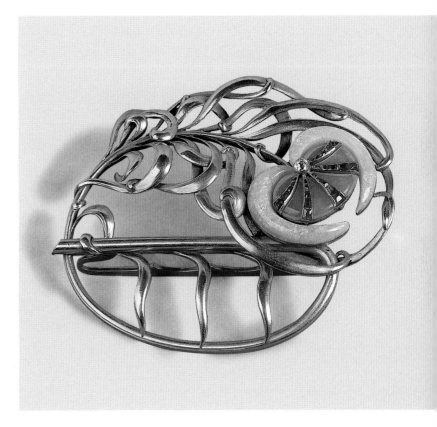

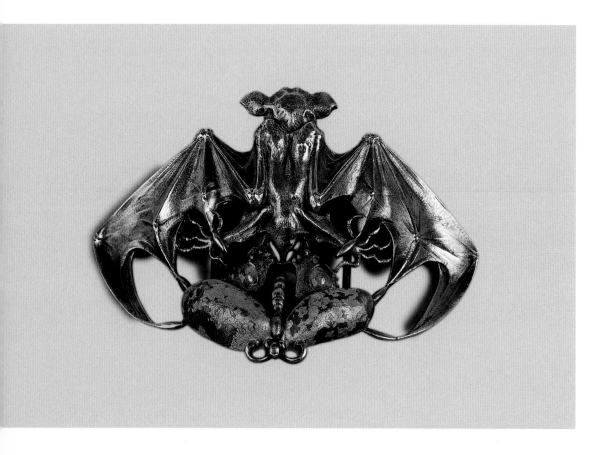

Gürtelschließe »Le Jour et la Nuit«
(Insekt und Fledermaus)
Silber, z.T. vergoldet, Amethyste
1897
Breite 12,5 cm
A.S.B.L. Philippe et Marcel Wolfers,
Brüssel

Belt buckle "Day and Night"
(Insect and Bat)
Silver, partly gilt, amethysts
1897
Width 12.5 cm
A.S.B.L. Philippe et Marcel Wolfers,
Brussels

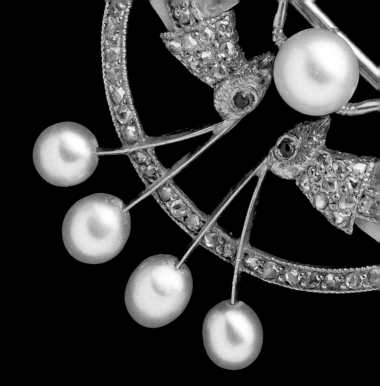

Lluis Masriera

Lluis Masriera

Lluis Masriera in seinem Atelier, 1904
Lluis Masriera in his atelier, 1904

Der Sohn und Enkel von Goldschmieden und Malern besuchte, selbst als Goldschmied, Emailleur und Schmuckentwerfer ausgebildet, die Weltausstellung 1900 in Paris. Lluis Masriera war damals achtundzwanzig Jahre alt, in Barcelona aufgewachsen im jahrzehntelang traditionell geführten Familienbetrieb. In Paris begegnete er der Schmuckkunst des Art Nouveau, die ihn nachhaltig beeindruckte. War es ein Schock, war es die pure Begeisterung – jedenfalls kam der junge Mann nach der (auch persönlichen?) Begegnung mit Lalique nach Barcelona zurück und veranlaßte, daß der gesamte konventionelle Schmuckbestand des Hauses *Masriera Hermanos* eingeschmolzen wurde. Im Jahre 1901 war die neue Kollektion nach Entwürfen von Lluis Masriera fertiggestellt; in einer Aus-

stellung feierte er – so wird berichtet – damit spektakuläre Erfolge.

Der neue Schmuck des Lluis Masriera fand die begeisterte Zustimmung in einer Stadt, die dem *Modernismo,* der katalanischen Variante des Jugendstils, verpflichtet war, in der Antonio Gaudí um 1890 mit der phantastischen Architektur der *Sagrada Familia* begonnen hatte, in der bildende Künstler, Musiker und Dichter den Aufbruch in eine neue Zeit betrieben. Lluis Masriera war Teil dieser Bewegung geworden mit seinen Schmuckkreationen, die trotz ihrer Verwandtschaft zum Art Nouveau eine ganz persönliche Note aufweisen.

Masriera hatte in Genf die verschiedenen Emailtechniken studiert. Das Fensteremail *(plique à jour)* hat er, glaubt man entsprechenden Berichten, für sich selbst neu entdeckt. Es spielt in Masrieras Schmuck mosaikartig angewandt eine bemerkenswerte Rolle und bestimmt in der delikat eingesetzten Farbigkeit und in exzellenter Verarbeitung den Charakter vieler Anhänger, Broschen und Zierkämme.

Wie in Paris sind die Vögel, die Libellen, die Frauen und die aus diesen Motiven symbolistisch kombinierten Wesen auch bei ihm häufig anzutreffen. Bemerkenswert ist, daß Masrieras Schmuck der in Paris dominierenden Plastizität weitgehend entbehrt. Viele seiner Anhänger sind eher flach konzipiert und beweisen so die Individualität des Katalanen. Lluis Masriera hat trotz der Affinität zum französischen Art Nouveau seinen ganz eigenständigen Beitrag zur europäischen Schmuckkunst um 1900 geliefert.

Lluis Masriera

His father and grandfather were goldsmiths and painters. Lluis Masriera trained as a goldsmith, enameller and jewellery designer and took part in the 1900 Paris Exhibition when he was twenty-eight years old. He grew up in Barcelona in the family business, which had been run for decades on traditional lines. In Paris Masriera was confronted with Art Nouveau jewellery design and the impact it made on him was instrumental in radically changing his approach to design. The young man returned to Barcelona after his encounter with Lalique (in person?). There he high-handedly had all the conventional jewellery cluttering the House of Masriera melted down. In 1901 a new collection based on Lluis Masriera's designs was ready for exhibition. By all accounts the opening night was memorable.

Lluis Masriera's new jewellery met with an enthusiastic response in the bastion of *Modernismo,* the Catalan variant of Art Nouveau. Barcelona boasts Antonio Gaudí's fantastic church of the *Sagrada Familia,* begun in 1890 and to this day defeating all attempts to finish it. Catalan artists, musicians and poets heralded the beginning of a new era with their own distinctive brand of Art Nouveau. Lluis Masriera became part of this movement with his imaginative jewellery.

Masriera studied enamel-working techniques in Geneva. He is said to have rediscovered *plique à jour* ("openwork fold"), which looks like miniature stained-glass windows. Used like mosaic, this technique figures prominently in Masriera's work, which is notable for extreme delicacy and translucency of colour. Masriera's mastery of plique à jour enamelling is evident in his pendants, brooches and ornamental combs.

Birds, dragonflies, ladies and beings combined in the Symbolist manner from two or more of these motifs are just as frequently encountered in Masriera's work as in Parisian Art Nouveau jewellery. However, Masriera's jewellery is notable for being almost devoid of the plasticity so admired in Paris. Many of his pendants were conceived as flat designs. Despite his obvious affinity with French Art Nouveau, Masriera's style is inimitably his own.

Blick in das Atelier von Lluis Masriera, Barcelona, 1904

A glimpse into Lluis Masriera's atelier, Barcelona, 1904

Lluis Masriera

Anhänger »Byzantinische Büste«
Gold, Elfenbein, Diamanten,
Saphire, Perlen, Email
um 1915
Länge 7 cm
Sammlung Masriera i Carreras, S.A.
(Grup Bagués), Barcelona

Pendant "Byzantine bust"
Gold, ivory, diamonds, sapphires,
pearls, enamel
ca 1915
Length 7 cm
Collection Masriera i Carreras, S.A.
(Grup Bagués), Barcelona

Lluis Masriera

Anhänger »Frauenbüste«
Gold, Diamanten, Perlen, Email
um 1913
Breite 5,5 cm
Sammlung Masriera i Carreras, S.A.
(Grup Bagués), Barcelona

Pendant "Bust of a woman"
Gold, diamonds, pearls, enamel
ca 1913
Width 5.5 cm
Collection Masriera i Carreras, S.A.
(Grup Bagués), Barcelona

Lluis Masriera

Anhänger »Landschaft«
Gold, Diamanten, Rubine, Perlen,
Email
um 1912
Länge 5 cm
Sammlung Masriera i Carreras, S.A.
(Grup Bagués), Barcelona

Pendant "Landscape"
Gold, diamonds, rubies, pearls,
enamel
ca 1912
Length 5 cm
Collection Masriera i Carreras, S.A.
(Grup Bagués), Barcelona

Lluis Masriera

Armreif »Reiher«
Gold, Diamanten, Rubine, Email
um 1903
Durchmesser 6 cm
Sammlung Masriera i Carreras, S.A.
(Grup Bagués), Barcelona
Abb. S. 116/117

Bangle "Heron"
Gold, diamonds, rubies, enamel
ca 1903
Diameter 6 cm
Collection Masriera i Carreras, S.A.
(Grup Bagués), Barcelona
ill. p. 116/117

Lluis Masriera

Anhänger/Brosche »Reiher«
Gold, Diamanten, Perle
um 1908
Länge 5 cm
Sammlung Masriera i Carreras, S.A.
(Grup Bagués), Barcelona

Pendant/brooch "Heron"
Gold, diamonds, pearl
ca 1908
Length 5 cm
Collection Masriera i Carreras, S.A.
(Grup Bagués), Barcelona

Lluis Masriera

Brosche »Reiher«
(ursprünglich wohl Zierstück eines
Schmuckkammes)
Gold, Diamanten, Rubine, Email
um 1902
Breite 9 cm
Sammlung Masriera i Carreras, S.A.
(Grup Bagués), Barcelona

Brooch "Heron"
(probably originally decorated a
comb)
Gold, diamonds, rubies, enamel
ca 1902
Width 9 cm
Collection Masriera i Carreras, S.A.
(Grup Bagués), Barcelona

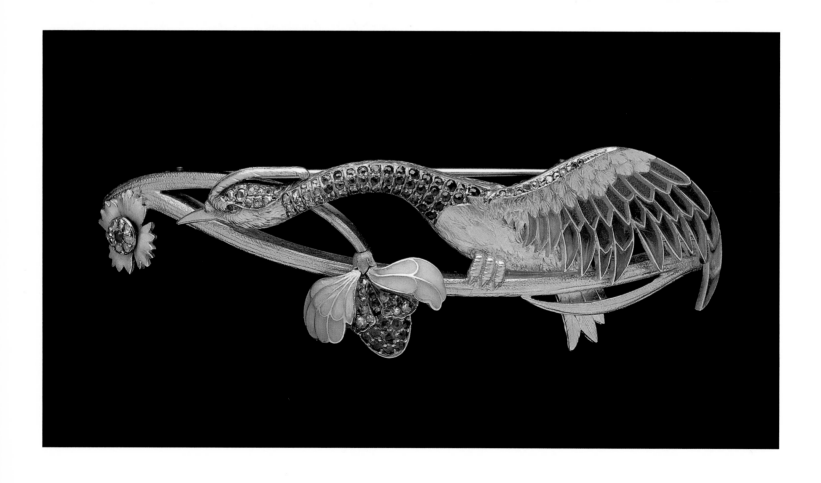

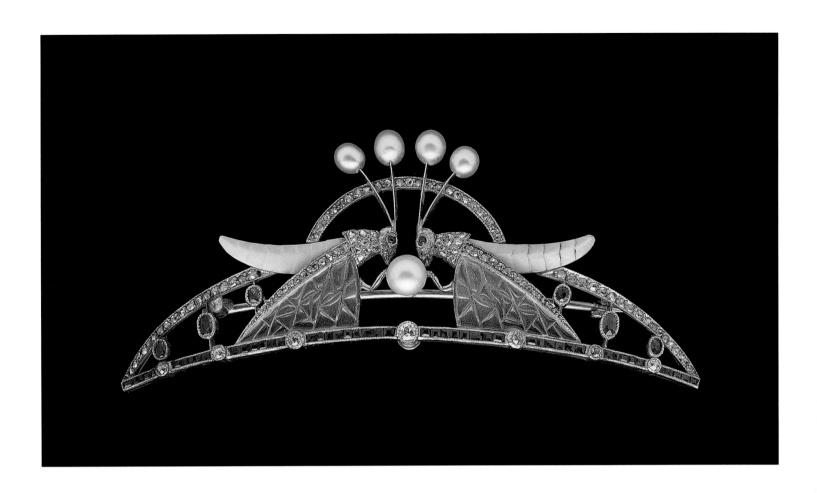

Lluis Masriera

Brosche »Zwei Libellen«
Gold, Diamanten, Rubine, Perlen,
Elfenbein, Email
1908
Breite 8,7 cm
Sammlung Masriera i Carreras, S.A.
(Grup Bagués), Barcelona

Brooch "Two dragonflies"
Gold, diamonds, rubies, pearls,
ivory, enamel
1908
Width 8.7 cm
Collection Masriera i Carreras, S.A.
(Grup Bagués), Barcelona

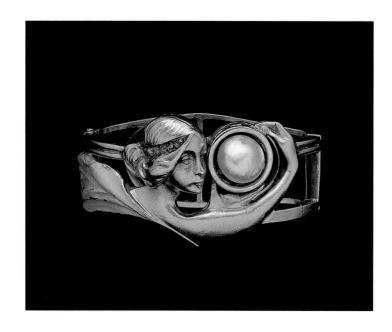

Lluis Masriera

Schalspange »Mädchen mit Perle«
Gold, Silber, Diamanten, Perle,
Email
nach 1901
Breite 3,4 cm
Sammlung Masriera i Carreras, S.A.
(Grup Bagués), Barcelona

Scarf slide "Girl with pearl"
Gold, silver, diamonds, pearl, enamel
after 1901
Width 3.4 cm
Collection Masriera i Carreras, S.A.
(Grup Bagués), Barcelona

Lluis Masriera

Armreif »Frauenfigur«
Gold, Diamanten, Email
zwischen 1909 und 1916
Breite 5,5 cm
Sammlung Masriera i Carreras, S.A.
(Grup Bagués), Barcelona

Bracelet "Figure of a woman"
Gold, diamonds, enamel
between 1909 and 1916
Width 5.5 cm
Collection Masriera i Carreras, S.A.
(Grup Bagués), Barcelona

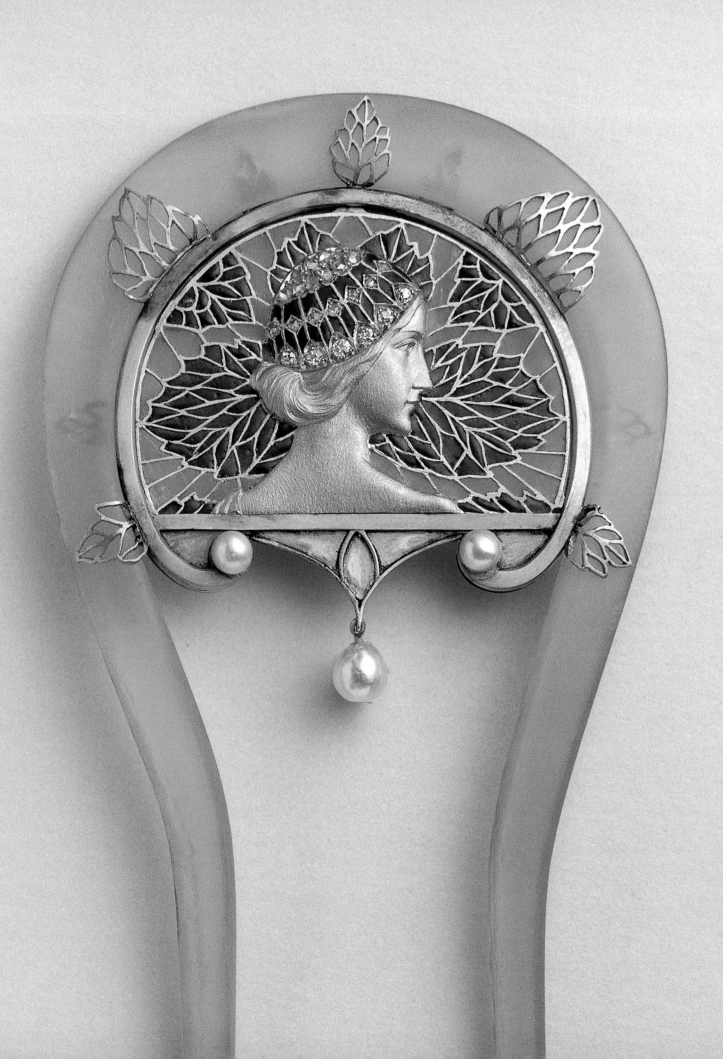

Lluis Masriera

Haarstecker »Frauenbüste«
Silber, z.T. vergoldet, Perlen,
Email, Horn
um 1910
Höhe 11,25 cm
Privatbesitz

Hairpin "Bust of a woman"
Silver, partly gilt, pearls,
enamel, horn
ca 1910
Height 11.25 cm
Private collection

Lluis Masriera

Haarstecker »Lilien«
Gold, Diamanten, Email, Schildpatt
um 1901/03
Höhe 12,7 cm
Sammlung Masriera i Carreras, S.A.
(Grup Bagués), Barcelona

Hairpin "Lilies"
Gold, diamonds, enamel,
tortoiseshell
ca 1901/03
Height 12.7 cm
Collection Masriera i Carreras, S.A.
(Grup Bagués), Barcelona

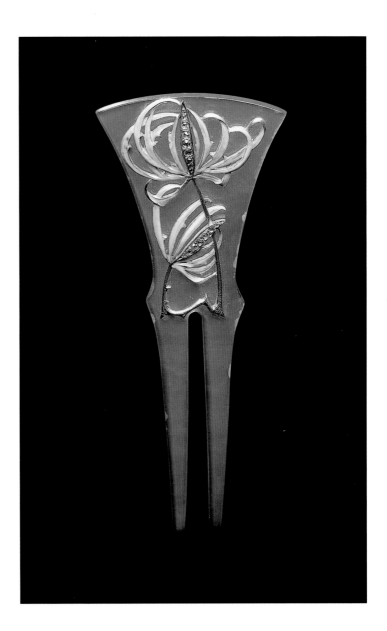

Lluis Masriera

Anhänger
Gold, Diamanten, Smaragde,
Email
Breite 4,5 cm
Moderne Nachbildung aus der
Masriera-Werkstatt in Barcelona
nach dem Original von 1912

Pendant
Gold, diamonds, emeralds, enamel
Width 4.5 cm
Modern replica from the Masriera
Atelier in Barcelona of the original
made in 1912

Lluis Masriera

Anhänger »Libellenfrau«
Gold, Diamanten, Perle, Email
Breite 6,5 cm
Moderne Nachbildung aus der
Masriera-Werkstatt in Barcelona
nach dem Original von 1901

Pendant "Dragonfly Lady"
Gold, diamonds, pearl, enamel
Width 6.5 cm
Modern replica from the Masriera
Atelier in Barcelona of the original
made in 1901

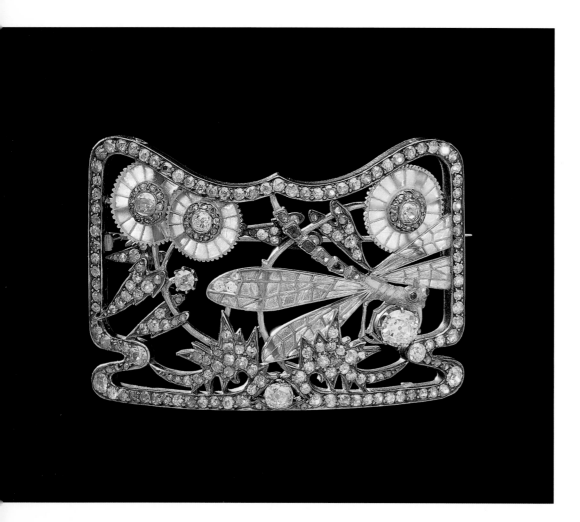

Lluis Masriera

Brosche »Libelle«
Gold, Silber, Smaragde, Rubine,
Email
um 1903/06
Breite 7 cm
Sammlung Masriera i Carreras, S.A.
(Grup Bagués), Barcelona

Brooch "Dragonfly"
Gold, silver, emeralds, rubies, enamel
ca 1903/06
Width 7 cm
Collection Masriera i Carreras, S.A.
(Grup Bagués), Barcelona

Wilhelm Lucas
von Cranach

Wilhelm Lucas von Cranach

Wilhelm Lucas von Cranachs Wappen mit Signatur

Wilhelm Lucas von Cranach's coat of arms with his signature

Viele Schmuckstücke, die der Berliner Künstler Wilhelm Lucas von Cranach entworfen hat, zeigen als Hauptmotiv eine oder mehrere Schlangen. Die geflügelte Schlange, der Drache, war das Wappentier seines berühmten Vorfahren, des Renaissance-Malers Lucas Cranach d. Ä.

Die Schlange, geflügelt wie bei einem der Cranachschen Anhänger, bei einigen seiner Fingerringe und indirekt bei der *Gorgoneion*-Brosche (Abb. S. 134/135), ohne Flügel bei Cranachs letztem Schmuckstück, dem *Schlangennest* (Abb. S. 132), war für ihn wohl in zweifacher Weise von Bedeutung: Zum einen in der Erinnerung an den Künstler der Renaissance und damit auch zur Identifikation des einen Cranach mit dem anderen, mehr noch in der Absicht, dieses Tier mit seinen durch die europäische Kulturgeschichte hindurch so vielfältigen und auch widersprüchlichen mythologischen und symbolischen Inhalten zur eigenen Deutung und persönlichen Aussage zu nutzen: Ist es doch nachweisbar, daß Cranach wie auch Philippe Wolfers, dem er freundschaftlich verbunden war, nicht nur ästhetische Werte und Gesichtspunkte ansetzte, sondern sich zu politischen und gesellschaftlichen Fragen seiner Zeit auszudrücken suchte.

Wenn im Zusammenhang mit dem Schmuckschaffen Cranachs die Schlange als ein »Träger unguter, verführerischer oder gewalttätiger Kraft« bezeichnet wird, so trifft ähnliches auf den Kraken zu, der in Cranachs Brosche *Tintenfisch und Schmetterling* (Abb. S. 131) bösartig in Erscheinung tritt, zum Symbol des Grausamen

wird und in seiner morbiden Schönheit im für diesen aussichtslosen Kampf mit dem Schmetterling ein »Beitrag zur ästhetischen Bewältigung des Schrecklichen« ist (Ulrike von Hase).

Ähnliches gilt auch für andere Schmuckstücke, die nach Entwürfen des ursprünglich zum Forstmann ausgebildeten Wilhelm Lucas von Cranach in den Ateliers der Berliner Juweliere Louis Werner und Gebrüder Friedländer entstanden sind. Seine *Gorgoneion*-Brosche ist ein beeindruckendes Zeugnis für die »Ästhetisierung des Grauens«, verbindet sie doch die raffinierte Schönheit in Entwurf und Ausführung mit dem Prinzip des Dämonischen.

Wilhelm Lucas von Cranach steht als deutscher Schmuckgestalter der Jahrhundertwende in einem besonderen Spannungsfeld. Er verwirklicht – ganz anders als die Franzosen, der Belgier und die Katalane und doch verwandt mit diesen – seine persönlichen Vorstellungen als individuelle Aussagen zu den Problemen seiner Zeit.

Wilhelm Lucas von Cranach

Pieces of jewellery designed by the Berlin artist Wilhelm Lucas von Cranach are notable for serpents as their principal motif. The winged serpent or dragon was on the coat of arms granted to his illustrious ancestor, the Renaissance painter Lucas Cranach the Elder.

The winged serpent featured in a von Cranach pendant, in rings and, as an ancillary motif, in his *Gorgon's Head* brooch (fig. pp. 134/135). The last piece of jewellery he designed is a *Nest of Serpents* (fig. p. 132), without wings. The serpent meant two things to von Cranach. It reminded the artist of the Renaissance and was, therefore, the significant link between him and his Renaissance ancestor. His intention was to use the serpent, associated as it had been down through history with so many, even contradictory, mythological and symbolic layers of meaning, as a vehicle for making his own statement as an artist. Like Philippe Wolfers, who was a friend of his, von Cranach approached art not only from the aesthetic standpoint but also as a medium for voicing opinions on the political and social issues of the day.

In connection with von Cranach's jewellery, the serpent is described as the "bearer of evil, seductive or violent forces". This is especially true of the cuttlefish or squid, which in von Cranach's *Octopus and Butterfly* brooch (fig. p. 131), appears as a malevolent creature, a morbidly beautiful symbol of cruelty. The outcome of the butterfly's struggle with it is a foregone conclusion. The cuttlefish motif in von Cranach's work represents a symbolic "contribution to overcoming terror by aesthetic means" (Ulrike von Hase).

This also applies to other pieces of jewellery made after designs by Wilhelm Lucas von Cranach in the ateliers of the Berlin jewellers Louis Werner and Gebrüder Friedländer. The von Cranach *Gorgon's Head* brooch attests impressively to a sophisticated aesthetic of the diabolic linked with mastery of design and execution.

As a German jewellery designer, Wilhelm Lucas von Cranach was at the confluence of several Fin de Siècle aesthetic currents. His work differs from that of his French, Belgian and Catalan contemporaries yet he reveals an affinity with them all because his designs invoke political and social ideas as well as aesthetic pronouncements.

Louis Werner, Court Jeweller • Berlin, Friedrichstr. 190 • Modern jewelry from designs by the artist Lukas von Cranach. 4513

Ausriß aus der Seite 351 des Kataloges »International Exposition Paris 1900, Official-Catalogue Exhibition of the German-Empire«, Berlin 1900

Excerpt from page 351 of the catalogue "International Exposition Paris 1900, Official-Catalogue Exhibition of the German-Empire", Berlin 1900

Wilhelm Lucas von Cranach

Anhänger »Geflügelte Schlangen«
Ausführung Gebr. Friedländer,
Berlin
Gold, Jade, Perle, Turmalin, Rubin,
Diamant
vor 1903
Breite 7 cm
Privatbesitz

Pendant "Winged serpents"
Execution Gebr. Friedländer, Berlin
Gold, jade, pearl, tourmaline, ruby,
diamond
before 1903
Width 7 cm
Private collection

Wilhelm Lucas von Cranach

Brosche »Tintenfisch und
Schmetterling«
Ausführung Louis Werner, Berlin
Gold, Diamanten, Rubine,
Amethyste, Topas, Perlen, Email
1900
Breite 8,3 cm
Schmuckmuseum Pforzheim

Brooch "Octopus and butterfly"
Execution Louis Werner, Berlin
Gold, diamonds, rubies, amethysts,
topaz, pearls, enamel
1900
Width 8.3 cm
Schmuckmuseum Pforzheim

Wilhelm Lucas von Cranach

Anhänger »Schlangennest«
Ausführung Gebr. Friedländer,
Berlin
**Gold, Diamanten, Smaragde,
Rubine, auf Perlmutt verwachsene
Perlen**
1917/18
Breite 3,6 cm
Schmuckmuseum Pforzheim

Pendant "Serpents' nest"
Execution Gebr. Friedländer, Berlin
Gold, diamonds, emeralds, rubies,
pearls on mother-of-pearl
1917/18
Width 3.6 cm
Schmuckmuseum Pforzheim

Wilhelm Lucas von Cranach

Anhänger/Brosche »Goldregen«
Gold, Perlen, Email
vor 1903
Länge 7,1 cm
Sammlung Barlow-Widmann,
München

Pendant/brooch "Laburnum"
Gold, pearls, enamel
before 1903
Length 7.1 cm
Barlow-Widmann Collection,
Munich

*Wilhelm Lucas
von Cranach*

Brosche »Gorgoneion«
Ausführung Gebr. Friedländer,
Berlin
Gold, Opal, Nephrit, Jaspis,
Diamanten, Perle
1902
Breite 13,7 cm
Staatliche Museen zu Berlin,
Kunstgewerbemuseum

Brooch "Gorgon's head"
Execution Gebr. Friedländer, Berlin
Gold, opal, nephrite, jasper,
diamonds, pearl
1902
Width 13.7 cm
Staatliche Museen zu Berlin,
Kunstgewerbemuseum

Wilhelm Lucas
von Cranach

**Schlangenring
(Verlobungsring
W. L. von Cranachs)
Gold, Saphire
1900
Durchmesser 2 cm
Privatbesitz**

Snake ring
(W. L. von Cranach's
engagement ring)
Gold, sapphires
1900
Diameter 2 cm
Private collection

Wilhelm Lucas
von Cranach

**Ring »Geflügelte Schlange«
Gold, Saphire, Email
vor 1903
Durchmesser 2,3 cm
Privatbesitz**

Ring "Winged serpent"
Gold, sapphires, enamel
before 1903
Diameter 2.3 cm
Private collection

Wilhelm Lucas von Cranach

Ring »Geflügelte Schlange«
Gold, Rubin
vor 1903
Durchmesser 1,9 cm
Privatbesitz

Ring "Winged serpent"
Gold, ruby
before 1903
Diameter 1.9 cm
Private collection

Wilhelm Lucas von Cranach

Ring »Zwei Löwen«
Gold, Saphir
nach 1900
Höhe 3,1 cm
Privatbesitz

Ring "Two lions"
Gold, sapphire
after 1900
Height 3.1 cm
Private collection

Wilhelm Lucas
von Cranach

**Schmuckkamm »Fabelwesen«
Horn, Gold, Diamanten, Rubine,
Smaragde, Perle, Email
um 1900/02
Höhe 14,3 cm
Bayerisches Nationalmuseum,
München**

Ornamental comb "Mythical
creature"
Horn, gold, diamonds, rubies,
emeralds, pearl, enamel
ca 1900/02
Height 14.3 cm
Bayerisches Nationalmuseum,
Munich

René Lalique

1860   in Ay an der Marne als Sohn
eines Handelskaufmanns
geboren.

1876 bis 1879   Goldschmiedelehre bei Louis
Aucoc in Paris; Studien an der
École des Arts Décoratifs in
Paris und am Sydenham College
in London.

1884   erstmalige, noch anonyme Ausstellung von Schmuckentwürfen
im Louvre.

1885   Übernahme einer Goldschmiede-
werkstätte in Paris; Anfertigung
von Schmuck für Pariser Juweliere.

1895   erstmalige Ausstellung unter
eigenem Namen im Salon der
Société des Artistes Français
in Paris; Beteiligung an diesen
Ausstellungen bis 1909.

seit 1897   Teilnahme und Einzelausstellun-
gen u.a. in Brüssel, München,
Turin, Berlin, London, St. Louis,
Lüttich und Sankt Petersburg.

1900   triumphale Beteiligung an der
Pariser Weltausstellung; Auszeichnung mit einem *Grand Prix*
und dem Orden eines Offiziers
der Ehrenlegion.

1905   Eröffnung eines neuen Ladengeschäftes an der Place Vendôme.

1908/09   Übernahme einer Glasmanu-
faktur bei Paris; von nun an
widmet sich Lalique mehr und
mehr und dann ausschließlich
dem künstlerisch gestalteten
Glas.

1945   stirbt René Lalique in Paris.

LITERATUR (neueste Publikation):
Ausstellungskatalog *The Jewels of Lalique*,
Paris/New York 1998

Georges Fouquet

1862   in Paris als Sohn des Juweliers
Alphonse Fouquet geboren.

Ab 1891   Mitarbeit im väterlichen
Juweliergeschäft.

1895   Übernahme des Betriebes.

1897   erstmalige Beteiligung am Salon
der Société des Artistes Français;
erregt dort 1898 die Aufmerksamkeit der Öffentlichkeit.

Seit 1899   intensive Zusammenarbeit mit
dem freiberuflichen Schmuckentwerfer Charles Desrosiers
und dem Maler und Grafiker
Alphonse Mucha.

1900   erfolgreiche Teilnahme an der
Pariser Weltausstellung; Goldmedaille für Schmuckstücke
nach Entwürfen von Mucha.

1901   Einrichtung eines neuen Laden-
geschäftes in der Rue Royale
(Entwurf von Alphonse Mucha).
In der Folge Beteiligung an zahl-
reichen Ausstellungen in Paris,
Lüttich, Mailand u. a.

1925   ist Georges Fouquet Präsident
der Sektion Bijouterie-Joaillerie
der Exposition Internationale
des Arts Décoratifs in Paris.

1957   stirbt Georges Fouquet in Paris.

LITERATUR: Ausstellungskatalog
Les Fouquet, Paris 1983
(deutschsprachige Ausgabe:
Die Fouquet, Zürich 1984)

Léopold Gautrait

Trotz vieler Versuche, mehr über
L. Gautrait in Erfahrung zu
bringen, bleibt dieser Schmuckkünstler des Art Nouveau weiter-
hin nahezu unbekannt. Die
neuere Forschung scheint zumindest nachzuweisen, daß Gautrait
nicht Lucien, sondern Léopold
mit Vornamen hieß. Als Lebens-
daten werden die Jahre 1865 bis
1937 angenommen. Weder seine
Herkunft noch seine Ausbildung
zum Schmuckentwerfer bzw.

Goldschmied sind bekannt. Die
Signatur auf Schmuckstücken,
die in der Werkstätte des Pariser
Juweliers Léon Gariod entstan-
denen sind, ist ein Hinweis auf
L. Gautrait, ein anderer ist die
Erwähnung durch Henri Vever
im dritten Band seiner *La Bijou-
terie Française au XIXᵉ Siècle*, wo
Gautrait als *ciseleur-modeleur*
und *fidèle collaborateur* von
Léon Gariod bezeichnet wird.

Lucien Gaillard

1861   geboren in Paris als Sohn des
Goldschmieds Ernest Gaillard.

1878   Beginn der Ausbildung zum
Goldschmied im väterlichen
Betrieb; Gaillard interessiert
sich stark für japanische Metall-
techniken.

1889   Beteiligung an der Pariser
Weltausstellung; Auszeichnung
mit einer Goldmedaille.

1892   Übernahme der väterlichen
Firma.

1900   Beteiligung an der Pariser
Weltausstellung; Auszeichnung
mit einem *Grand Prix*.

Ab 1900   verstärktes Interesse an der
Kunst Japans: Beschäftigung
japanischer Kunsthandwerker in
seinen im Jahre 1900 neu ein-
gerichteten großen Werkstätten.

1901 bis 1909   Teilnahme an den Salons der
Société des Artistes Français in
Paris mit Auszeichnungen.

1933   stirbt Lucien Gaillard in Paris.

LITERATUR: Ausstellungskatalog
Pariser Schmuck, München 1989
(mit ausführlichen Literaturangaben)

La Maison Vever

1821 gründet Pierre Vever sein Juweliergeschäft in Metz.

1870 verläßt dessen Sohn Ernest
Lothringen und erwirbt in Paris
die Firma Baugrand.

1850 wird Paul Vever, 1853 sein Bru-
der Henri geboren, die 1874 in
die Firma des Vaters eintreten
und 1881 die Geschäftsführung
übernehmen.

1878 und 1889 Teilnahme an den Weltausstel-
lungen in Paris; Auszeichnung
mit einem *Grand Prix;* in der
Folge Beteiligungen an Ausstellungen in Moskau, Chicago und
Brüssel.

1900 großer Erfolg bei der Pariser
Weltausstellung, im besonderen
mit Schmuckstücken nach Entwürfen des aus der Schweiz
stammenden Eugène Grasset
(1841–1917).
Henri Vever betätigt sich als
Kunstschriftsteller und gibt
1906 bis 1908 sein dreibändiges
Werk *La Bijouterie Française au
XIXe Siècle* heraus.

1915 stirbt Paul Vever in Paris.

1921 übergibt Henri die Maison Vever
an seine Neffen André und Pierre
Vever.

1942 stirbt Henri Vever in Paris.

LITERATUR: Ausstellungskatalog
Pariser Schmuck, München 1989
(mit weiteren Literaturangaben)

Philippe Wolfers

1858 in Brüssel als Sohn des aus
Deutschland übergesiedelten
Gold- und Silberschmieds
Louis Wolfers geboren.

1874 Teilnahme an Kursen für Bildhauerei und Zeichnen an der
Académie Royale des Beaux-Arts
in Brüssel.

Ab 1875 Ausbildung in der väterlichen
Gold- und Silbermanufaktur.

1892 Übernahme des Betriebes zusammen mit seinen Brüdern
Max und Robert; Philippe ist
der künstlerische Leiter.

1894 Beteiligung bei der Weltausstellung in Antwerpen.

1900 stellt Philippe Wolfers anläßlich
der Pariser Weltausstellung
in der Galerie Aublanc in Paris
aus; er ist stark beeindruckt von
Laliques Arbeiten.

Bis 1907 entstehen noch vereinzelt
Schmuckstücke; Wolfers konzen-
triert sich mehr und mehr auf
die Bildhauerei.

1909/10 entsteht in Brüssel nach Entwurf
von Victor Horta ein neues
Geschäftshaus der Firma Wolfers
Frères.

1929 stirbt Philippe Wolfers in
Brüssel.

LITERATUR: Ausstellungskatalog *Philippe
& Marcel Wolfers, De l'Art Nouveau à l'Art
Déco,* o.O. 1992
Ausstellungskatalog *Philippe und Marcel
Wolfers,* Zürich 1993

Lluis Masriera i Rosés

1872 in Barcelona als Sohn des Malers
und Goldschmieds Josep
Masriera i Manovens geboren.
Ausbildung zum Goldschmied
im 1839 gegründeten Familienbetrieb.

1889 Studium der Emailtechniken
an der Kunstakademie in Genf
bei Edouard Lossier.

1897 Beteiligung an der Exposición
General de Bellas Artes in
Madrid mit Gemälden und
einigen Schmuckstücken.

1900 die auf der Pariser Weltausstellung gezeigten Schmuckstücke
von René Lalique üben einen
großen Eindruck auf Lluis
Masriera aus.

1901 zeigt er erstmals anläßlich einer
Ausstellung im Hause Masriera
seinen vom Art Nouveau beein-
flußten Schmuck.
In den folgenden Jahren konti-
nuierliche Teilnahme an Ausstellungen, u.a. in Barcelona,
Madrid, Paris, Buenos Aires,
Saragossa, Mexiko; Masriera
wird mehrfach ausgezeichnet.

1958 stirbt Lluis Masriera in Barcelona.

LITERATUR: Ausstellungskatalog
Els Masriera, Barcelona 1996

Wilhelm Lucas von Cranach

1861 in Stargard/Pommern geboren.
Ausbildung als Forstmann.

1886 Studium der Malerei an der
Kunstschule in Weimar.

1892 Kunststudium in Paris.

Seit 1893 lebt von Cranach in Berlin.
Neben der Malerei und Archi-
tekturentwürfen betätigt sich
von Cranach als Entwerfer
für Schmuck; Zusammenarbeit
mit den Berliner Juwelieren
Louis Werner und Gebrüder
Friedländer.

1900 Beteiligung an der Pariser Weltausstellung mit dem von Louis
Werner ausgeführten Schmuckstück »Tintenfisch und Schmetterling« (S. 131).

1902 aufsehenerregende Beteiligung
an der Ausstellung zum 25jähri-
gen Bestehen des Vereins für
Deutsches Kunstgewerbe zu
Berlin mit von der Firma Gebrüder Friedländer ausgeführten
Schmuckstücken.

1903 veröffentlicht Wilhelm Bode
das Tafelwerk *Werke moderner
Goldschmiedekunst von
W. Lucas von Cranach.*

1918 stirbt Wilhelm Lucas von
Cranach in Berlin.

LITERATUR: Ulrike von Hase, *Schmuck
in Deutschland und Österreich 1895–1914,*
München 1977

René Lalique

1860   Born in Ay, Marne, the son of a businessman.

1876–1879   Trained as a goldsmith under Louis Aucoc in Paris; studied at the École des Arts Décoratifs in Paris and at Sydenham College, London.

1884   First (still anonymous) exhibition of jewellery designs in the Louvre.

1885   Took over a goldsmith's atelier in Paris; worked as a freelance making jewellery for Paris jewellers.

1895   First exhibited work under his own name in the Salon of the Société des Artistes Français in Paris; showed at these annual Salons until 1909.

From 1897   Took part in exhibitions and had one-man shows in Brussels, Munich, Torino, Berlin, London, St. Louis, Liège and St Petersburg.

1900   Triumph at the Paris Exhibition; awarded a *Grand Prix;* given the Legion of Honour.

1905   Opened a new shop, Place Vendôme.

1908/09   Took over a glass factory near Paris; from now on increasingly concerned with making art objects of glass, to which he ultimately devoted himself entirely.

1945   René Lalique died in Paris.

REFERENCES (latest publication): Exhibition catalogue *The Jewels of Lalique,* Paris/New York 1998

Georges Fouquet

1862   Born in Paris, the son of the jeweller Alphonse Fouquet.

From 1891   worked in his father's jeweller's shop.

1895   Took over the business.

1897   Participated for the first time in the Salon of the Société des Artistes Français; attracted the public's notice there in 1898.

From 1899   Worked closely with the freelance jewellery designer Charles Desrosiers and the painter and graphic artist Alphonse Mucha.

1900   Successful at the Paris Exhibition; gold medal for jewellery after designs by Mucha.

1901   Opened a new shop in the rue Royale (designed by Alphonse Mucha). Later successes at numerous exhibitions in Paris, Liège, Milan, etc.

1925   Georges Fouquet became president of the Section Bijouterie-Joaillerie at the Exposition Internationale des Arts Décoratifs in Paris.

1957   Georges Fouquet died in Paris.

REFERENCES: Exhibition catalogue *Les Fouquet,* Paris 1983 (German edition: *Die Fouquet,* Zurich 1984)

Léopold Gautrait

All attempts to uncover more about L. Gautrait notwithstanding, nothing is really known about this Art Nouveau artist and jewellery-maker. Recent research seems to have uncovered evidence that Gautrait's first name was Léopold and not Lucien as originally thought. His birth and death dates are assumed to be 1865 to 1937. It is not known what his origins were nor where, how and even if he trained as a jewellery designer. The signature on pieces of jewellery made in the ateliers of the Paris jeweller Léon Gariod would seem to indicate L. Gautrait. A further trace of this elusive jewellery designer and maker is a brief mention in the third volume of Henri Vever's *La Bijouterie Française au XIXᵉ Siècle.* There Gautrait is described as a *ciseleur-modeleur* and *fidèle collaborateur.*

Lucien Gaillard

1861   Born in Paris, the son of the goldsmith Ernest Gaillard.

1878   Began training as a goldsmith in his father's firm; Gaillard was already interested in Japanese metal-working techniques.

1889   Participated in the Paris Exhibition; awarded a gold medal.

1892   Took over his father's firm.

1900   Exhibited work at the Paris Exhibition; awarded a *Grand Prix.*

From 1900   Increasingly preoccupied with Japanese art; employed Japanese artisans in the new, large ateliers he opened in 1900.

1901–1909   Exhibited at the Salons of the Société des Artistes Français in Paris, where he won awards.

1933   Lucien Gaillard died in Paris.

REFERENCES: Exhibition catalogue *Pariser Schmuck,* Munich 1989 (with comprehensive bibliography)

La Maison Vever

1821 Pierre Vever founded a jewellery shop in Metz.

1870 His son Ernest left Lorraine for Paris, where he bought the firm of Baugrand.

1850 Paul Vever and his brother Henri, born in 1853, entered their father's business in 1874, taking over the management of it in 1881.

1878 and 1889 Participated in the Paris Exhibitions; awarded a *Grand Prix;* followed by participation in exhibitions in Moscow, Chicago and Brussels.

1900 Great success at the Paris Exhibition with jewellery after designs by Eugène Grasset, a Swiss (1841–1917).
Henri Vever was active as an art critic and his three-volume work *La Bijouterie Française au XIXᵉ Siècle* was published 1906–1908.

1915 Paul Vever died in Paris.

1921 Henri handed over Maison Vever to his nephews, André and Pierre Vever.

1942 Henri Vever died in Paris.

REFERENCES: Exhibition catalogue *Pariser Schmuck,* Munich 1989 (with further references)

Philippe Wolfers

1858 Born in Brussels, the son of Louis Wolfers, a German gold and silversmith who had emigrated to Belgium.

1874 Took courses in sculpture and drawing at the Académie Royale des Beaux-Arts in Brussels.

From 1875 Trained in his father's gold and silver business.

1892 Took over the business together with his brothers Max and Robert; Philippe was design

manager.

1894 Exhibited at the Antwerp Exhibition.

1900 Philippe Wolfers exhibited at the Galerie Aublanc in Paris during the Paris 1900 Exhibition; he was highly impressed by Lalique's work.

Until 1907 Still made individual pieces of jewellery; Wolfers increasingly concentrated on sculpture.

1909/10 The new offices of Wolfers Frères built in Brussels after plans by Victor Horta.

1929 Philippe Wolfers died in Brussels.

REFERENCES: Exhibition catalogue *Philippe & Marcel Wolfers, de l'Art Nouveau à l'Art Déco,* n. p. 1992
Exhibition catalogue *Philippe und Marcel Wolfers,* Zurich 1993

Lluis Masriera i Rosés

1872 Born in Barcelona, the son of the painter and goldsmith Josep Masriera i Manovens. Trained as a goldsmith in the family firm, founded in 1839.

1889 Studied enamelling techniques at the Geneva art academy under Edouard Lossier.

1897 Exhibited paintings and pieces of jewellery at the Exposición General de Bellas Artes in Madrid.

1900 Lluis Masriera greatly admired jewellery exhibited by René Lalique at the Paris Exhibition.

1901 First exhibition of his own work, influenced by Art Nouveau, in the firm of Masriera.
In the following years regularly showed work at exhibitions in Barcelona, Madrid, Paris, Buenos Aires, Saragossa, Mexico; Masriera received several awards.

1958 Lluis Masriera died in Barcelona.

REFERENCES: Exhibition catalogue *Els Masriera,* Barcelona 1996

Wilhelm Lucas von Cranach

1861 Born in Stargard, Pomerania, trained in forestry.

1886 Studied painting at the Weimar art academy.

1892 Studied art in Paris.

From 1893 Lived in Berlin.
Cranach painted and drew plans for architects in addition to designing jewellery; collaborated with the Berlin jewellers Louis Werner and Gebrüder Friedländer.

1900 Showed the piece of jewellery he designed and Louis Werner made called 'Cuttlefish and Butterfly' at the Paris Exhibition (page 131).

1902 The pieces of jewellery made by Gebrüder Friedländer on the 25th anniversary of the Verein für Deutsches Kunstgewerbe in Berlin created a sensation.

1903 Wilhelm Bode published *Werke moderner Goldschmiedekunst von W. Lucas von Cranach* with plates reproducing his work.

1918 Wilhelm Lucas von Cranach died in Berlin.

REFERENCES: Ulrike von Hase, *Schmuck in Deutschland und Österreich 1895–1914,* Munich 1977

Literaturverzeichnis ·
Bibliography

Ausführliche Literaturhinweise bis 1989
in Katalog
Complete bibliography up to 1989 in exhibition catalogue

Pariser Schmuck, Vom Zweiten Kaiserreich
zur Belle Epoque, München 1989

Besonders zu empfehlen sind
Selected references

Sigrid Barten, René Lalique. Schmuck und
Objets d'art 1890–1910, München 1977

Vivienne Becker, Art Nouveau Jewelry,
London 1985

Sigrid Canz, Symbolistische Bildvorstel-
lungen im Juwelierschmuck um 1900,
Dissertation München 1976

Alastair Duncan (Hrsg.), The Paris Salons
1895–1914 Jewellery, 2 Bände, London
1994

Ulrike von Hase, Schmuck in Deutschland
und Österreich 1895–1914, München 1977

Ulrike von Hase-Schmundt, Jugendstilschmuck. Die europäischen Zentren,
München 1998

Katalog Die Fouquet – Schmuckkünstler in
Paris, Zürich 1984

Katalog René Lalique – Bijoux, Verres,
Paris 1991

Katalog The Jewels of Lalique, Paris/
New York 1998

A. Kenneth Snowman (Hrsg.), The Master
Jewelers, London 1990

Henri Vever, La Bijouterie Française au
XIXᵉ Siècle, Band III, Paris 1908 (Reprint
Florenz)

Personenregister ·
Index of Names

Alle Seitenangaben beziehen sich auf den
deutschen Text.
All page numbers refer to the German text.